The Online Identity Theft Prevention Kit

Stop Scammers, Hackers, and Identify Thieves from Ruining Your Life

Vincennes University
Shake Learning Resources Center
Vincennes, In 47591-9986

The Online Identity Theft Prevention Kit: Stop Scammers, Hackers, and Identify Thieves from Ruining Your LIfe

Copyright © 2008 Atlantic Publishing Group, Inc.
1405 SW 6th Avenue • Ocala, Florida 34471 • Phone 800-814-1132 • Fax 352-622-1875
Web site: www.atlantic-pub.com • E-mail: sales@atlantic-pub.com
SAN Number: 268-1250

ISBN 13: 978-1-60138-008-1   ISBN 10: 1-60138-008-9

The online identity theft prevention kit : stop scammers, hackers, and identity thieves from ruining your life.
   p. cm.
 ISBN-13: 978-1-60138-008-1 (alk. paper)
 ISBN-10: 1-60138-008-9 (alk. paper)
 1. Identity theft--United States. 2. Identity theft--United States--Prevention.

HV6679.O65 2008
362.88--dc22

2008001975

Interior Layout: Vickie Taylor • vtaylor@atlantic-pub.com

Printed in the United States

Printed on Recycled Paper

With special thanks to Allison Boyer
for her help in compiling this book.

We recently lost our beloved pet "Bear," who was not only our best and dearest friend but also the "Vice President of Sunshine" here at Atlantic Publishing. He did not receive a salary but worked tirelessly 24 hours a day to please his parents. Bear was a rescue dog that turned around and showered myself, my wife Sherri, his grandparents Jean, Bob and Nancy and every person and animal he met (maybe not rabbits) with friendship and love. He made a lot of people smile every day.

We wanted you to know that a portion of the profits of this book will be donated to The Humane Society of the United States.

–Douglas & Sherri Brown

THE HUMANE SOCIETY OF THE UNITED STATES ©

The human-animal bond is as old as human history. We cherish our animal companions for their unconditional affection and acceptance. We feel a thrill when we glimpse wild creatures in their natural habitat or in our own backyard.

Unfortunately, the human-animal bond has at times been weakened. Humans have exploited some animal species to the point of extinction.

The Humane Society of the United States makes a difference in the lives of animals here at home and worldwide. The HSUS is dedicated to creating a world where our relationship with animals is guided by compassion. We seek a truly humane society in which animals are respected for their intrinsic value, and where the human-animal bond is strong.

Want to help animals? We have plenty of suggestions. Adopt a pet from a local shelter, join The Humane Society and be a part of our work to help companion animals and wildlife. You will be funding our educational, legislative, investigative and outreach projects in the U.S. and across the globe.

Or perhaps you'd like to make a memorial donation in honor of a pet, friend or relative? You can through our Kindred Spirits program. And if you'd like to contribute in a more structured way, our Planned Giving Office has suggestions about estate planning, annuities, and even gifts of stock that avoid capital gains taxes.

Maybe you have land that you would like to preserve as a lasting habitat for wildlife. Our Wildlife Land Trust can help you. Perhaps the land you want to share is a backyard—that's enough. Our Urban Wildlife Sanctuary Program will show you how to create a habitat for your wild neighbors.

So you see, it's easy to help animals. And The HSUS is here to help.

The Humane Society of the United States
2100 L Street NW
Washington, DC 20037
202-452-1100
www.hsus.org

TABLE OF CONTENTS

SCARY STATISTICS: IS THE INTERNET REALLY SAFE?

In 2007, United States consumers lost an estimated $3.2 billion in online credit card fraud, according to a study done by Celent Communications. $3.2 billion.

The Federal Trade Commission estimates that ten million Americans have their identity stolen or misused every year. 10 million every year.

One of the major U.S.-based consumer research firms estimated that one of the most common online scams, phishing, alone costs consumers $929 million in 2005. Did you get that? $929 million.

The statistics are scary, and as the Internet gets more and more popular, these statistics are only going to rise

— unless consumers everywhere begin to work together to take a stand against online identity theft. The best way to make the journey to a more secure future is with a guide, and this online identity theft prevention kit is your map, so to speak. It may sound a bit cliché, but knowledge really is power. Until you understand the threats out there on the never-ending World Wide Web, you cannot stop the criminals that want to take advantage of you and your personal information, and until we can stop these crooks, consumers everywhere will lose a ton of money every single year.

How much money? Billions. Let us look at some more statistics:

- Americans spend $1.7 trillion in the medical industry every year. Fraud accounts for up to 10 percent of that money — billions and billions of dollars.

- Crime cost banks and other financial institutions in the United States $33 billion in 1998. That statistic has only risen over this past decade.

- The average consumer loses over $2,400 in an identity theft. That is not counting the damage it does to your credit and reputation.

- The average business loses over $10,000 in an identity theft.

- In 2005, almost 50 people lost over $1 million during their identity theft problems.

A stolen identity can be sold for some quick cash or used for any number of things, such as getting a job, running from the cops, or opening credit card accounts. Some people do not have a day job; they just steal identities. Others are able to work part-time or seemingly live beyond their means. Still others can enter this country illegally with a stolen identity or commit crimes in your name. Anyone you meet, from your son's new girlfriend to your gardener to the guy in the online forums who private messaged you, is a potential threat. Paranoia will get you nowhere. Instead, you have to think fast and act faster, all while continually protecting yourself and your information.

LEARNING ABOUT PREVENTION IS PREVENTION: BE THE FAST ZEBRA

There is some good news in all this: Identity thieves do not like hard targets. The whole goal of stealing identities is to collect information as fast as possible to make as much money as possible. If you remember even half of the identity theft prevention tips listed in this book, you will be a much harder target, and the amateur identity criminals, which constitute at least 50 percent of all thieves out there, will pass you by. Therefore, the first step of prevention is to learn about prevention.

Did you buy this book online? As silly as it sounds, that in and of itself may have already helped fend off an attacker. On the chance that an identity thief tried to access your account wherever you bought this book, seeing that you are interested in catching people just like him or her is a natural deterrent. With millions of Internet users, why would you go after someone who is taking an active interest in putting you behind bars? There are plenty of fish in the sea.

Statistically, it simply makes the most sense to go after the easy targets. Think of yourself as a zebra and the identity thief as a hungry lion. Now, a lion does not just run to the group of zebras and attack. No, the lion plans carefully and watches all the animals, looking for the weaker links. When zebras sense that a lion is in the area, they begin to run, and the lion will pick off the slowest and weakest. There is no sense in struggling to kill a larger, faster, stronger animal, in the lion's mind, and he is right. If a lion goes after a fast zebra, he may miss his target, resulting in no meal at all. The weaker zebra is obviously the better choice. Prevention tips are like speed to zebras. Every tip you learn will make you a little faster and a little stronger. If you are at the head of the pack, most identity thieves will pass you up and go after the other, more weakly protected identities instead.

And if that does not make sense to you, think about it this way: If nothing else, prevention tips will make you a savvy consumer. You will be able to spot identity theft sooner, contact the right people more quickly, and bring the culprits to justice. Every identity thief behind bars is one less criminal crippling the Internet for the rest of us.

While this book is a good start for identity theft, keep in mind that the world of thievery on the Internet is changing constantly. Therefore, you need to keep up the defense at all times. You are a fast zebra now – do not get out of shape!

HOW WE GOT HERE: A BRIEF HISTORY OF IDENTITY THEFT

Identity theft is nothing new. One can almost imagine cave men pretending to be one another to get a mate or sleep in the best cave dwellings. In fact, there are cases of identity theft in very early religious texts, such as the Old Testament of the Bible. In the book of Genesis, which is one of the oldest in the entire Bible, Jacob pretends to be his brother, Esau, and tricks his near-blind father into granting him a handsome birthright. This was probably not the first case of one person pretending to be another, but it does illustrate a good point – identity theft is usually about money or rights. Today, things are no different, although someone does not have to be physically blind to be blind to a destructive identity theft.

Identity theft really exploded, however, with the use of the credit card. Credit cards were first proposed in the late 1800s, with the first working models being used in the 1930s. However, at this time, credit card usage was very,

very limited, so using them for a means of identity theft was next to impossible. However, in the 1950s, the Diner's Club became the first mainstream credit card used by the general public, followed shortly by original first versions of the Visa. Less than a decade later, MasterCard joined the scene, and soon, many credit card options were available.

However, until the 1980s, using a credit card was cumbersome. The clerk had to verify that you were allowed to use the card by searching through a large book of numbers to make sure you were in good standing or by calling the card company and verifying your number. Credit cards were impractical, and prone to identity theft, as huge books of names and numbers were published for use in most of the major stores in the country. Identity thieves simply had to be smart about it to steal a credit card number. Unfortunately, once they had it, they could be easily and quickly caught, since there really weren't many credit cards in use.

The swipe machine with instant verification made identity theft more lucrative, but also a bit harder. The use of credit cards rose considerably, and by 1995, over half of all American households owned a credit card. With the mainstream popularity of the Internet, these figures have been on the rise even more, since purchasing items on the Internet is most often done through using a credit card. Between one half and three quarters of all identity theft cases in general include the misuse of a credit card. Millions of people have become victims of identity theft since they were first put to use over half a century ago.

And it is not only about credit cards. The history of identity theft spans multiple tracks, with people using a number of methods to steal your identity online. Stealing your credit card information is just the start. Savvy Internet thieves learn how to steal all sorts of private information about you, including the mother of all private identification numbers, your social security number.

WHO IS STEALING IDENTITIES?

Identities stolen online often bring to mind the picture of a computer nerd spending hours late into the night creating complex computer programs. In reality, most computer nerds would rather be leveling up on Final Fantasy or worshipping their copy of Halo 3. Most online identity thieves are not the stereotypical computer brains with no friends and no lives. With a faceless crime such as this, there really is no norm. You just cannot assume that identity thieves are lurking in dark corners. White-collar criminals come in all shapes and sizes, and most are not nearly as sinister-looking as your mind wants you to believe.

Victim information shows that over 25 percent of all identity theft victims know their attacker. That means if your identity is stolen, there is a one in four chance that an acquaintance, friend, or family member did it. Yes, I said family member. Thousands of relatives actually steal the identities of their children, parents, siblings, cousins, and grandparents every year. You may think you know your spouse well, but they are not immune to becoming identity thieves either. However, most of these cases do not involve online actions. If a family member wants to steal your identity, it is most likely that he or she will do so the old-fashioned way — by actually taking your credit card, your social security card, or other piece of vital information. Regardless of how it is done, identity theft within the family is a big problem.

Beyond your family, trusting others should be even more difficult for you, especially when your personal information is involved. Studies on identity theft have proven that about 70 percent of all cases are insider jobs, meaning that the employee of a company with your information is the person who wants to steal your identity most. Want an even scarier statistic? Many of these insider jobs were done by the CEO, president, or business owner. Your information just is not safe.

Check out the following descriptions. Can you tell which of the following ten descriptions are of people who committed identity theft in the past? Take this quiz and see how you do. Be sure to check Appendix 2 for the answers.

1. Mark and Nancy Shae are a fun couple, running an adult business online. They built up online friendships over the course of a few years, participating in a number of online forums and message boards. Suddenly, Nancy announces that Mark has passed away. She has to shut down her online sites to prepare for the funeral and pay her other expenses. A few of the other people on the forums suggest that a group of you band together to help. After all, Mark and

Nancy have been good friends and have great sites. They set up a memorial fund of sorts where members can donate to help Nancy pay for funeral expenses, and they ask anyone with Web design experience to donate time to help keep the sites operating. Do you help out?

2. You are a leader in the computer industry, and a young man from Seattle calls you to tell you that he is working on a whole new networking system for your products. He makes promises that this could change the world and wants you to hire him, giving him access to your products. This self-proclaimed computer genius is a college student with no real course of study, but does have a background in technology and amazing SAT scores. Do you agree to meet for a product demo and possible sponsorship?

3. Scott, 45, from Boca Raton, Florida owns a company that specializes in online advertising. He works with clients from around the world and contacts your company to see if you are interested in this innovative new product. According to Scott, the company has already compiled a list of people who are potentially interested in your product. Do you decide to work with Scott?

4. You decide to get a new job and apply at one of the world's largest retail stores. After a lengthy application process, you are denied on the grounds that they

already had your social security number on file. You have never worked there before, but they assure you that there has probably been a mistake, and they will look into the matter as soon as possible to correct the faulty employee number in their records. In the meantime, they recommend that you apply to other stores, but they will call you if you become eligible after the mistake is cleared. What do you do?

5. You log online and join a Christian dating site, where you meet a number of nice men. One in particular stands out, and you begin exchanging e-mails back and forth to get to know one another. The conversation gets more and more passionate, and you look forward to reading his e-mails every day. You decide to plan a face-to-face meeting. However, the man is a construction worker and in another country at the moment building a sports stadium, so he asks you to wait for him. You agree, and in the next few months you receive multiple gifts from your suitor, including a bouquet of balloons that says "I love you" sent to your office. He is set to come home in a few weeks, and you cannot wait to meet your soul mate. Suddenly, there is a problem. He is having a hard time cashing his checks for the return trip home since he is in Africa and asks if you could do him a favor. Would you cash the check and wire him the money? You are hesitant, but you agree. In a few days, you feel duped because you have sent him the money but the bank has called and there was a problem with the check. You confront him about it and he feels horrible. He will be home in a few days, though, and will straighten this out. You talk about moving in together and how great it will be to finally sort out the money mess and get to know one another. Do you continue to trust him, even after the problem?

6. You have tried the bar scene and, although you have met plenty of women, cannot seem to find that special one. While it is a bit embarrassing and you do not tell any of your friends, you sign up on some online dating Web sites and begin to browse the other profiles. After a few weeks, you meet a very cute girl online, and after some e-mails back and forth for a little less than a month, she wants to meet up with you. Do you trust her and go on the date?

7. After battling a number of health problems, you are told by your doctor that you should consider a number of medications to help. However, these medications are all very expensive and you opt instead to simply try to make do. In the next few months, your condition only worsens — but so does your financial situation. You cannot even afford to see your doctor again, as you have no health insurance coverage. You go online to see if there are any home remedies or non-prescription drugs available to help you, and you find an online pharmacy that will consult with you and help you buy drugs at a fraction of the cost. It seems legitimate. You are asked to fill out a form

about your condition, which will then be reviewed by a medical staff to see if you qualify. If you do, you can get generic versions of the drugs you need without an official prescription, and they will cost a lot less. You fill out the application, noting your symptoms and past treatment, and in less than a week you have been approved. Do you order the online medications at a low price?

8. Larry was one of the country's first PhD students in the field of computer sciences. He is an average-looking guy with a five o'clock shadow and a love for building new programs. After studying programming for a few years, he begins to develop a new program that scans Web sites all over the Internet, leaving no stone unturned. He decides to quit school and focus on this project full-time, realizing that this new technology could bring in millions. Larry understands computers better than just about anyone else in the whole world, and he asks you if you would like to invest in his little project. Do you?

9. It is your son's first day of soccer practice and the coach informs you that, in order for your son to play, you must release his social security number and health insurance information. It seems like a valid need, but does make you a bit uneasy, especially since the coach asked for the number in a quick e-mail to you. Your son really wants to play soccer, and a call to the school confirms that, to play, the coach does need the social security number in case

your son is hurt while you are not there or cannot be contacted. Do you trust the coach?

10. You and your spouse finally have enough money saved up to purchase a house. You begin looking at a few properties and decide to contact a real estate agent to help you find the perfect house. She shows you a few, and you are surprised at just how expensive real estate can be. However, she also tells you that she can work out a deal with a lender rather quickly and, being on a tight budget, you choose a house in the downtown area. It needs a few repairs, but the realtor and her lawyer show you the documentation that the house has been inspected and the information from the lender that you have been approved for the loan. Should you sign the paperwork and buy the house?

The stats below may surprise you – these are the people who are really stealing your identity, according to numerous studies done by the Federal Trade Commission, the Social Security Administration, and private protection agencies:

- About 60 percent of identity thieves are people who do not know you. That means the other 40 percent are people who do know you – family members, co-workers, neighbors, friends, or other acquaintances.

- The vast majority of identity thieves (over 70 percent) have no prior criminal record. For many, they are not even running scam rings – this is their first offense.

- While most identity thieves are males, women account for about one-third of all cases, which is a much higher percentage than most other crimes.

- An overwhelming majority of people are not stealing identities because they need drug money. In fact, drug-related identity theft crimes account for less than 3 percent of all identity theft cases.

- When businesses are attacked, it is only done by an insider about 30 percent of the time. Over time, an outside source finds a loophole and attacks.

As you can see, the numbers are really general. If we had a hundred identity thieves in a room together, you would know 40 of them and not know 60 of them. 30 of them would have been in trouble with the law before, but 70 of them would be first-time offenders. Thirty-three of them would be women and 67 of them would be male. You cannot really draw conclusions from those characteristics at all – identity thieves really can be almost anyone.

That does not mean that we should be paranoid. In general, only a small percentage of the population is trying to steal your identity. However, it does mean that you have to be smart. You have to know that absolutely everyone in your life – from your teenage son to your next door neighbor to your drycleaner – is a potential identity thief. Do not let paranoia take over your life, but at the same time, do not share information with everyone you meet.

The fastest growing crime in both the United States and the United Kingdom is identity theft. In 2006, the Federal Trade Commission registered over 650,000 consumer fraud complaints in the U.S.

2

WHY WOULD ANYONE WANT MY IDENTITY ANYWAY?

"But who would want to be me?"

That is the question most identity theft victims struggle to answer. It makes sense — if you were given the chance to be anyone in the world, would you not want to be a movie star or some other high-profile, glamorous person? With identity theft, however, remember that a person is not actually becoming you in real life. They are simply becoming you on paper. They just want to use you to make a little money. If you are not famous, you are a much better target because you probably have not paid a team of financial advisors and Internet experts to protect you from people that want to steal your identity. The more "plain Jane" you are, the better.

There are basically two ways in which your identity will be used once it is stolen:

1. The person who steals a piece of your information can sell it for $10 to $500 (depending on who you are) to someone else who will use it.

2. An "end user" gets your information, either by stealing it directly or by buying it from someone who has stolen it, and it can then be used in a number of ways.

In either case, using your identity is illegal, but extremely beneficial for criminals. It comes down to one of two things: money or avoiding the law. When your identity is stolen, your life can be ruined. Prevention starts with understanding how your identity can be used. Let us do a quick quiz. How do you think criminals can use your identity? Which of the following scenarios do you think are potential threats and which are purely fictional events that could never happen?

- A waiter hands you the check and you pay with a credit card. On the way to the cash register, he swipes it through a small machine on his belt loop that looks like a pager. This "pager" records the number and your other card information, and at the end of the week, the waiter sells the pager for a few hundred dollars. Is this threat real or fictional?

- Someone steals your wallet in which you have been carrying your social security card. She then uses that number to help an illegal immigrant friend get a job and apartment in your name. Is this threat real or fictional?

- A college student studying computer programming steals your laptop. He is able to retrieve files that you deleted a few months ago. These files contain the password to your online bank account, which he proceeds to drain. Is this threat real or fictional?

- Using stolen information, a thief figures out your social security number. He then uses it to get a driver's license and eventually is arrested and flees his bail. The police show up at your door, guns drawn, to take you back to jail. Is this threat real or fictional?

- Someone steals your mail and uses a free credit card offer to apply for credit in your name. In less than a week, you are thousands of dollars in debt. Is this threat real or fictional?

- Your child signs up for little league, and the coach says he needs his social security number for insurance reasons. You fill out the form, and the coach files it in his home office. The coach's brother takes the pile of forms and assumes your child's identity to open bank accounts, take out loans, and avoid the police. Is this threat real or fictional?

How did you answer? You might be surprised to find out that all the above scenarios can and do happen to many people every day. Your identity is not safe, and once it has been stolen, it can be used in many ways. Do not fall into a trap of believing that it cannot happen to you.

After all, your identity is a hot commodity. It does not matter if you are not beautiful, do not have that Mercedes or have been passed up for a promotion at work. Identity thieves do not care who you are. They just care that you are an easy target. You might not know that your identity has been stolen for years — decades even — or you might figure it out right away. Either way, the thief has made a quick buck, and when you steal hundreds of identities, you make enough money to support yourself on that alone. Identity theft is the fastest-growing white-collar crime in America, and that is why it is so important to stop being the easy target.

MAKING A QUICK DOLLAR BY SELLING IDENTITIES

The fastest way to make money by stealing identities is to be the collector. Collectors do not actually want to use the identities. They just want the money. There are thousands of people willing to pay as much as $500 for your identity, so these criminals decide to cash in on this gold mine. Even for something as easy to collect as your name, address, and credit card number, collectors can make $10. Say you collect even just ten numbers a day. That is $700 per week and approximately $2,800 per month. Without even trying, identity thieves can be well on their way to quitting that office job or going on that dream vacation.

Another reason why this is appealing is that, if you are caught, you will be slapped on the hand a bit and let go. Sure, a second or third offender is going to get jail time, but in many states, the laws for selling important information are fairly lax. These thieves can rest easy knowing that, if they are somehow identified as an identity thief, they can simply leave the life of crime with few consequences. In fact, most of the people caught for selling information actually enter plea bargains. In exchange for information regarding the people buying the identities, they are released with little more than a few fines.

On top of that, it is hard to catch these collectors. Imagine that you begin to see some suspicious activity on your credit card. The charges were made online from an IP address in Boston and a car was registered in your name in a neighboring state. That is where you will first look to find the scammer. However, there is a chance that the waiter you met while on vacation in Hawaii was actually the person who stole your information. He simply sold it to someone on the east coast of the United States. Stopping the end user will be your number one priority, and unless you catch that thief and he or she tells you about the supplies (if that information is even known), you will never think to look in Hawaii for a culprit.

Even if you do find the next person in the chain, he or she may not have been the person to collect your information.

Your credit card number may have passed through multiple channels to get to Boston. Maybe the first person just wanted to use your credit card information to open a store card account. The second person may have used it to access your PayPal account. The third person may have done something completely different. Everyone buying and selling along the way shares in the risk of getting caught, but few people will actually know where the card originated. To them, you are just another number.

The collector can really use any of the methods listed in this book as a way to steal your identity and sell it for profit. However, the quickest and most efficient way to go about collecting a large volume of numbers without any additional work is through skimming. Skimming is a practice in which your credit card is scanned quickly though a non-confidential device, which is then hooked up to a computer to retrieve data. I mention skimming here because this is strictly an offline offense. It is the real world equivalent to the virtual spyware or spoofed Web site.

THE END USER – HOW CAN AN IDENTITY BE USED?

At the end of the line, someone has to use the identity. Otherwise, it would not be worth any money. Your credit card number, social security number, or other crucial information may be bought and sold a number of times before it finally reaches the person who is going to use it — the end user. An end user is putting the most on the line in terms of risk, but even if he or she pays $500 or more for a single piece of information, the rewards are great. One identity could bring in thousands or even millions of dollars. Beyond money, the end user can also use your identity for a number of other reasons as well.

According to experts, identity theft falls into four distinct categories:

1. Financial

2. Criminal

3. Cloning

4. Commercial

Each has its own kinds of end-users who want different things out of your identity. In some cases, the person who steals you identity can use it in more than one of the above ways in order to get the most money for your information. In other words, if there is a problem with your identity once, chances are that there will be lots of places where your personal information shows up across the country – or even around the world.

Opening Accounts and Clearing Out Accounts

One of the most common ways a thief can use your identity is to open up new credit card accounts or take out new loans. What exactly the thief does really depends on the amount of information he or she is willing to buy, as well as the time that he or she is able to devote to covering his or her tracks. There is the guerilla approach, or there is the long-term approach, depending on the goals of the thief.

The guerilla approach is to open as many accounts in your name as quickly as possible and then to make as much money as possible before disappearing. This all happens within a month, if not more quickly. After all, the bills will still come to you, and most people will call to report the problem the second they start getting huge bills for things they never bought — or even from cards they did not know they had. This type of thief does not have much time, but because credit card limits usually start at around $2,000, even opening five cards means a profit of $10,000 or more. How is that for a day's work?

This can become easier and easier because credit card companies now have programs where you can pull cash from your card through ATMs or even cash checks made to yourself to pull money from the card. Purchases can be more easily tracked, but once the money is pulled, you will have a hard time tracking it down again. An identity thief will not use the ATM around the corner from his house. He or she may mail the card to an accomplice thousands of miles away or use the card while on vacation. Once the money is in a thief's pocket, it is hard to reclaim it.

All someone really needs to get started is your credit card number, the expiration date, and the security number, which is found on the back of the card. Therefore, anyone who picks up your card can make a note of these numbers, which can then be used online to purchase any number of things. Thieves use public computers to avoid IP address tracking and have the items shipped to a PO Box, which can be registered under a false name and closed after the purchase is received. They can also cover their tracks by transferring money with the card to another account, like their online PayPal account. The more they bounce the money around, the easier it is to get lost in the shuffle. As they transfer the money and close accounts along the way, they hope that police will eventually reach a dead end and give up. Sadly, this is usually the case. A few thousand dollars may be financially devastating to you, but it is not enough money to justify police involvement for long if that case gets cold.

Someone who is willing to pay a bit more for a better piece of information — your social security number — can make even more money with the guerilla technique, because that allows them to open up new accounts in your name. Sometimes, you do not even need a social security number to do this. Do you receive pre-approved credit card offers? Thieves can dumpster dive, fill them out, and send them in, using a PO Box address. In less than two weeks, they will have a shiny, new card — or maybe five shiny, new cards — all in your name. Until you get that first month's bill, you will have no idea what is going on.

Of course, if the thief has the card itself, it is even less work to steal from you. Gas pumps do not need a signature, and most cashiers never compare signatures or check identifications like they are supposed to be doing. Unless you miss your card right away, a thief can get away with a lot of charges in a relatively short amount of time. They will usually discard your credit card in 48 hours, since you are likely to report it missing, which puts a flag on the card.

Credit card accounts are not the only thing that should worry you. Identity thieves can also use your personal information to take out loans quickly. This is a much trickier thing to do, but it has happened in the past. In addition, thieves can open bank accounts, which they can use for illegal purposes. That way, if they are caught, they can just disappear, leaving you holding the ball.

If you have online accounts, these are most at risk for identity theft. You do not even need to know a person's name to steal this kind of money — all you need is a screen name and password. By using spoofing, phishing, hacking, and spyware scams, thieves can easily trick you into releasing your information. In a matter of moments, they can drain your money into their own account and close your account, making it even harder for you to catch them. Unless you have your account information written down, you may not even have a number to give to the people you call for an inquiry. All you know is that you cannot get into your account, and all they know is that you do not technically have an account anymore. Every day you spend on the phone trying to work out the problem, it gets harder and harder to actually catch the person who committed the crime.

There is another approach to the opening accounts technique, but this is much, much less common. This technique is usually used with people who, for some reason, cannot open their own accounts. In many cases, it has to do with either bad credit or immigration (see below). In any case, they want to use your identity for a long, long time if they can, so they will make payments on time and work slowly so you will rarely find out that this is going on. Actually, if they do take out loans and repay them on time, this could help your credit — but I would not count on it. There is a reason they needed your identity to open an account in the first place.

Co-signers

Identity theft for co-signing falls into the same category as opening accounts, but the result is a bit different. Someone you know, often a spouse, child, or parent usually commits this type of identity theft, making it a personal, hurtful situation. Depending on the account and how the thief handles the situation, you could get lucky and actually have the theft help your credit. However, this best-case scenario does not happen often. It is much more likely that your credit will be damaged or the thief will begin to take more liberties with your identity, using some of the other mentioned methods.

Understanding why one of your friends or family members needs your identity to act as a co-signer is rather simple — no weird uses here. The person simply needs to purchase something, for whatever reason, but cannot get funding without a co-signer. Usually, this is because the person in question has poor credit. Using your identity, he or she forges the signature and releases your social security number. "You" are co-signing for an account you may not even know exists. In some cases, an identification number, like your social security number, is not needed; all it takes is a forged signature and some key information, like your birthday. For this reason, you need to always be aware of your credit score and credit history report.

Yes, someone stealing your identity could actually help your credit and you may never find out. This will only happen if the person who stole your identity does not fall behind on payments and pays off the debt quickly. However, it is likely that he or she will fall behind. Again, keep in mind that there is a reason why a co-signer is needed. If he or she were responsible and reliable with finances, a co-signer would not be needed. Furthermore, if he or she were trustworthy, there would be no need to steal your identity. You would just agree to be a co-signer honestly.

Fortunately, clearing up a co-signer theft is quite easy, because you can clearly prove that your signature was forged. In some cases, the thief will have an accomplice who pretends to be you when signing a contract in person or pretends to be you on the phone. In both cases, it is also easy to use a photo ID like your driver's license to show that someone else impersonated you.

Unfortunately, however, co-signer identity theft is a bit harder to catch. Usually, the lender will have a fake phone number on file for "you." So, you will not get called right away if there is a problem. Since most defaulted borrowers attempt to avoid lenders and collection agencies, this does not seem unusual in any way to the lender, and because you are just the co-signer and not the main person on the loan, your credit will probably be affected differently as well. This means you may not notice the differences right away on your credit score, especially if you have missed payments on your own loans, opened new accounts, and so forth. It may be easy to clear up co-signer identity theft, but it is not easy to catch it in the first place.

Using Your Name

Related to opening accounts and co-signing, an identity thief can use your name for other purposes as well. Imagine, if you will, that the identity thief has fairly bad credit but really wants a cell phone. In order to be approved, he or she uses your good name to establish credit. This works with just about any kind of account. When we think of identity thieves opening accounts in our names, we tend to think just of those thieves who open credit cards and max them out. However, account opening can go much, much deeper.

How else can an identity thief use your identity? Your name is not always about money. Sometimes, it is about authorization. Do you have access to certain things that other people do not? This is especially true in relation to your job. Government officials have to be extremely careful with passwords and personal information. Think about it – in spy movies, the good guys and the bad guys are always gaining access to "top secret" locations because they steal swipe cards or dress up like people who have access. It works that way in real life too. If you have access to some thing people want, they will stop at nothing to attempt to steal the information needed for that access.

On a more personal level, identity theft may just be about using your name. Many identity theft victims know their attackers, and although it is often about money, sometimes it is simply about a good name. For example, say you are a top professor in your field at a local college. One of your students, who has not exactly been a model scholar, has decided to try to get into grad school. Knowing that you will probably not write a very flattering letter of recommendation, he steals a document with your signature on it, writes his own letter, copies your signature, and sends it off. He also lists fake contact information for you so that everything is routed to his own cell phone. Then, he can pretend to be you on the phone. This may not be damaging to your finances, but it is damaging to your reputation when someone you seemingly recommended with bells and whistles turns out to be a horrible candidate for the grad school.

Get Out of Jail Free

Getting pulled over stinks. Imagine, though, that you have a few pounds of illegal drugs in the car and you see those flashing lights behind you because you have been speeding. You have about a second to make a choice: Either pull over and hope they do not notice or try to outrun the cops. Both situations are looking pretty bad to you right now.

Now imagine that you have a fake license and registration. You have registered the car in this fake name (or stolen it from the real owner), and you even have a fake social security number that matches the name on your license. Sure, you are inconvenienced. You will probably spend the night in jail until someone posts bail, and you will definitely lose whatever drugs were in the car, along with the car itself and your personal possessions. However, once you step out of the courtroom, you can simply disappear. Think of Joe Smith's surprise in a few months when the police knock on his door to arrest him for not showing up in court. I bet the cops will be even more surprised to see that Joe Smith is an 80-year-old man who has no idea what they are talking about. You, on the other hand, are a few states away and already setting up a new life under a new name.

Having a fake identity is a luxury for criminals everywhere. Even if you slip up, you have a get out of jail free card in your back pocket. That is worth a few hundred dollars, right? All you need to get started is a name, address, driver's license number, and social security number, and you can create almost any document you need to "be" someone else. The police will not know that you are not who you say you are until it is too late, and in the meantime, you can also use this information to open credit card accounts, buy items with loans, and even get a job.

Most of the criminals who use your identity for this purpose are not the people who actually steal it. Again, it passes through a number of hands before getting to the end user in most cases. In fact, the person who uses your identity probably knows nothing about you, other than your sensitive information. They do not know if you are a doctor with three kids or a deadbeat with no job. All they know is that you are someone that can help them get out of trouble fairly easily.

Unfortunately for you, that means that you have to spend time and money proving that you weren't the Joe Smith originally arrested for the crime. In most cases, this is done by comparing you to "your" mug shot taken the night of the crime. However, at times, this can be inconclusive, meaning that you have to go as far as proving your whereabouts when the incident took place. There may even be a court appearance with the arresting officer to further prove that you aren't guilty. Remember, in large cities, officers may arrest dozens of people every night. If you look remotely like the man or women they arrested, it will be hard to positively identify you as an identity theft victim.

Terrorism

Today, every country in the world has to worry about terrorism. The September 11, 2001 attack on the World Trade Center proved that no one is immune to the grip of unrelenting terrorism. In a perfect world, people everywhere would get along, but different religious, cultural, and economic values create conflict. War can be scary, but terrorism is by far scarier, as it thrives on fear and power. You could be helping terrorism rear its ugly head. Yes, you read that right. You, or more specifically your identity, could make it possible for terrorists to carry out horrible acts of terrorism.

There a quite a number of ways that terrorists can use your identity to help their causes. They may use your identity for just one of these reasons, or they mean use your identity to completely make their plans possible. The worst part about this is the very terrorist your identity helps to fund may directly hurt you and your loved ones. Here are just a few of the ways terrorists can use your personal information:

- **Financial Backing:** Like traditional identity thieves, terrorists who steal your identity can use it to empty out your bank accounts, open credit cards in your name, and otherwise steal money. They can then use this money to fund any number of terrorist plans. While terrorists often gather funding from followers, stealing identities is an even better option, as it means that there are no connections between followers and terrorist leaders.

- **Identity Cloning for Travel:** Suspected terrorists are usually red flagged so that they cannot travel easily. However, by using a copy of your personal information, they can create all of the documents they need to travel from country to country. It is fairly simple for someone with the right information and the technical skill to create a social security card, a passport, a birth certificate, a driver's license, and just about any other document you might need to travel within a country and worldwide. Insider sources have revealed that some terrorist organizations have five or more identities waiting and ready to go for each organization member. Not only will they use a fake identification, but they will use a number of fake identities. That way, they cannot be stopped and there is no record of travel by a single person. They will throw people off track however they can. Your identity is disposable.

- **Authorization:** Some special identities can have even more bearing on certain individuals. If you have access to something that terrorists want, you will be a special target for them. Really, who knows what they want. In some cases, they may want access to a specific physical area. In other cases, they will use your personal information to look like you on paper so that they will have access to a computer file. In still other cases, they want access to be allowed to do something, like order products only available to professionals or write prescriptions. Whatever the case may be, they will look for identities that have the authorization they need, and they will attempt to steal them.

Medicinal Uses

Identity theft can hurt you in ways other than financially. One of the most dangerous and damaging ways someone can steal your identity is for medical purposes. This really could be a matter of life and death. Like with almost every form of identity theft, the criminal can use your personal information in a simple fashion and discard it in a week, or the criminal can use your personal information for years, carefully covering his tracks so you never find out about it. Every situation is a bit different, depending on the thief's particular needs and wants.

Signatures are the most basic form of identity. If the goal is prescription drugs, forging doctors' signatures is the first step. However, this also involves creating fake phone numbers, fake addresses, and so forth. In any case, forging signatures of prescriptions is difficult, but the payoffs can be great. Prescription drug prices can be inflated ten times (or more) when sold on the streets.

There are quite a number of techniques that can be used to forge signatures, but in most low-level cases, it can be done simply by practicing and making your signature look close to that of the person you are intimidating. In most cases, the person requesting your signature will not be a trained specialist – "close" is all they need to allow you to pass. In the case of medical concerns, however, the signature does not mean much unless it is on a prescription pad, and can be confirmed with a call-in. This of course makes the process much, much harder for thieves. Nevertheless, it can still be done with a little planning.

Sometimes, doctors themselves cannot be trusted. Such was the 1999 case of Pennsylvania "doctor" David

Tremoglie, for example. Tremoglie posed as a psychiatrist for a number of years, treating over 500 patients and writing thousands of prescriptions before eventually being exposed as a fraud who had no medical license. Every year, there are thousands of cases like this from across the country — of people assuming the identities of doctors using stolen identities, forged signatures, or botched records. Sometimes, doctors themselves also become the criminals. Here is just a sampling of a few other cases in recent years:

- In Michigan, scammer Dennis Roask used a fraudulent medical license for over ten years. He treated thousands of patients and was involved in over 200 medical surgeries, including a number of heart bypass operations.

- In the 1970s, pharmacist Gerald Barnbaum's license was revoked. In response, he changed his name to Gerald Barnes, the same name as a prominent surgeon in California. He then proceeded to contact the real doctor's alma mater, asking for a copy of his license, as his had been destroyed. He used these documents to wreak havoc, destroying the real doctor's credit on a spending spree and practicing medicine in a number of clinics in California. As a result, some patients even died because the phony physician was not medically trained to make a proper diagnosis. He was eventually caught, but when released from jail years later, did the same thing all over again.

- In August of 2007, Dr. Trudi Shiu Newell of Sacramento was arrested for driving while under the influence of drugs. While investigating, police found that she also had a number of prescription pads from other doctors in her car and home. It is likely that Newell was assuming the other doctors' identities to write out multiple prescriptions, although the case is still pending.

- In 2005, a doctor in Philadelphia was arrested on suspicions of stealing patients' personal information. According to reports, he used credit card numbers, social security numbers, and home addresses to purchase items. He also stole information from co-workers at the Thomas Jefferson University Hospital, according to police. The damages totaled over $13,000 for the victims involved.

- Anil Mehandru of New York stole the name and Medicaid number of a doctor he scammed in a fake job interview in 1988. Mehandru billed almost $250,000 for medical services he did not use. In fact, Mehandru did not even pretend to be a doctor — he simply called in the charges from his one-room office.

Health insurance is another goal of identity theft that deals with the medical world. If you do not have health insurance, medical care can be extremely expensive. In fact, thousands of people across the nation do not get the care they need because they cannot afford it. Health insurance can help deter these costs, but if you cannot get it through your employer, it can be hard for a working family to afford decent coverage. The solution? Identity theft.

Does your health insurance card have your social security number written on it, or is your policy number the same as your social security number? Identity thieves are hoping that this is the case. By stealing your health insurance information, they can get the care they need on your dollar. It is common for family members to assume identities as well as for strangers to attempt to steal this personal information. Some thieves, once they have your social security number and other personal information, like your address, even open health insurance accounts. This is common if the thief needs a specific one-time treatment. After a month, you will get the bill in the mail and be alerted of the problem, but in a month's time, the thief can really rack up some hefty medical expenses.

Do not feel bad for the people who cannot afford health insurance and resort to stealing yours either. Victims often find out that their health insurance was used to pay for cosmetic treatments like nose jobs and breast enhancements. The danger here is that victims may have a spending limit per year, and if an identity thief uses a chunk of that money, the victim will be in trouble if he or she gets hurt and needs medical attention.

This scenario can also be extremely dangerous. Whenever you go to the doctor, whether it is through health insurance or not, your charts are updated to reflect current and past medical conditions. Allergies, medical preferences and aversions, and pre-existing conditions are all listed in your file. When two or more people share the same identity, the file is not accurate for anyone. You could receive lethal medical treatment because of an identity theft. If you know your identity is stolen, therefore, it is important that your doctor be one of the people you call.

Lastly, identity theft in the medical world can be used for avoiding the law, just like when a thief is arrested. Imagine this scenario: Jane is pregnant, but she has been using illegal drugs, which will show up in her blood work. She already has two children at home and is receiving child support payments for these children, as well as welfare for the entire family. Being busted for drugs is a quick way to have your children taken from you and put into foster care where they cannot earn you child support money. She will also lose her state-funded help and her record will land her in jail, in rehabilitation, or with heavy fines to pay. Yet Jane needs to have her baby delivered in a sterile environment, or she puts herself and the newborn at risk. Even the worst mother in the world wants to save herself.

The answer to this problem is identity theft. If Jane arrives at the hospital with a fake driver's license and fake social security number, the doctors will really think that she is Susan, the lady that baby-sits Jane's children from time-to-time. The doctors do notice that Jane has drugs in her system, and they press charges. However, when the police show up at Jane's home in a few days to arrest her, they do not find a baby or anyone that fits the description of Jane.

They are, in fact, at Susan's house. Still, they take her in for testing and questioning, and it is now up to Susan to prove that she was not the lady in the hospital. She recognizes the description of Jane, but it is too late — Jane skipped town immediately after having the baby. Unfortunately for Susan, the theft leaves a lot of questions unanswered, and her own children could be taken away until the matter is cleared. It is a sticky situation, and although Susan will not be responsible for any of Jane's hospital bills, her medical records are incorrect, her health insurance premiums may have risen, and her credit has probably been damaged. Let us not forget that Jane is still out there, using drugs, with a newborn and two other children that most likely need medical attention.

Someone wanted by the police, worried about violating parole or otherwise in a desperate legal situation, like Jane, is willing to pay for a new identity. If they cannot steal the information they need, they will pay a collector to give them what they want. It is just another step in the chain of stolen identities. If they work quickly enough, they can resell your information to someone else.

Immigration

If your identity is not used for financial reasons, then it will most likely be used for immigration reasons. There are thousands of illegal immigrants in the United States at any given time, and without valid citizenship, they will be deported or, at the least, they cannot really do much in the way of working, renting a place to live, or obtaining a driver's license. Immigrant identity thefts are some of the most profitable endeavors, but more people want to move to the United States every year, so business is booming.

When it comes to illegal immigration, it is most often your social security number that it at risk, and, in most cases, this number is used to get a job. Illegal immigration is all about flying below the radar, which makes it extremely hard to ever catch someone using your identity for immigration purposes. In fact, millions of people in the United States are using stolen social security numbers, and most of their victims have no idea. Unless there is a problem, you may not know for years.

Let us start at the beginning when it comes to identity theft and immigration. Immigrants first need to get into the country. This can be approved legitimately in a few ways, but most common is that someone will sponsor the immigrant as a spouse, fiancée, child, or other family member. Immigration is also possible for employment. In any case, it is becoming increasingly harder for immigrants, especially from some countries, which means that more and more people are resorting to illegal immigration. Unfortunately, your identity is put at risk when immigrants turn to desperate measures.

There are two main reasons people immigrate. First, it could be to reunite with family. The other reason? Better life opportunities. In other words, immigrants want to be safer, have more choices for a career, enjoy certain freedoms that their own country does not allow, and be able to choose better education. Looking at this reason more closely, what it really comes down to is money, and in the United States, you cannot work unless you have an identification number. You can get a work visa, but an easier route is to simply steal someone's identity.

Immigration identity theft is hard to catch because most are not focused on actually "getting ahead" and using your identity to make their millions. They just want to work. So, your identity will not be used, in most cases, to open credit card accounts, apply for loans, and so forth. It will just be used to get an honest job. The hope of most immigrants is to make a better life for their children and to live in peace, not to become instantly rich.

Sometimes, people who steal your identity will sell a bundle of information to an illegal immigrant. This person can totally assume your identity and, of course, this kind of theft is personally the most dangerous. It is also especially difficult to prove you are who you say you are when someone else also seems to have documentation proving that he or she is that person. With immigration, however, most people do not have the time, money, or ambition to steal your identity on this level. In fact, they do not want to — it is much riskier, and getting caught is never a good thing. Instead, the immigrant will just purchase your social security number. The name and other specifics do not matter most of the time.

Some immigrants do not even "steal" your social security number; they just make one up. In other words, when it gets to that line on the job application, an immigrant can just fill in whatever numbers he or she wants, and by chance, it could be yours. Some immigrants even use numbers that are clearly fake, such as 123-45-6789 or 111-22-3333. Thousands and thousands of employees are getting away with this every day because their employers just never check up on the validity of these social security numbers. Illegal immigrants are often cheap labor, so it is easy to look the other way.

Many immigrants seek the use of children's social security numbers because they are especially hard to catch. Your infant does not have a bank account or a job, so why would you check his or her credit report? That is exactly what identity thieves are hoping you are thinking. An illegal immigrant can get a solid 15 years (or more) out of a child's number without getting caught. After the child grows up and gets to be old enough to start wondering about weird credit implications or notices caused by the illegal immigrant, the number will be tossed and a new infant will become victim.

Better yet are social security numbers for dead people. No one really checks up on those, so they are perfect targets. It is also easier for an identity thief to steal social security numbers from dead people. Relatives in charge of executing an estate are often extremely sloppy with how the social security number is used. Most do not know their own legal rights or the rights of the deceased either. So, it is easy for a thief to run down a list of the obituaries, contact relatives, and say they are from, well, whatever phony agency they want to create. You would be surprised at how many people will willingly give out the social security number of their deceased loved one. Few realize the damage that can be done.

In any case, once an immigrant uses a stolen or "made up" social security number, you would think that the victim would be notified, right? Wrong. Most of the time, there is no indication by the Social Security Administration or Internal Revenue Service that your social security number has been misused. There are simply too many cases with which to deal. Because the procedures are so misconstrued, it is too hard to notify everyone, identify the real and fake users, and do much more than note on the record that there may be a problem.

In other words, you will never know. Here is generally what happens: Around tax time, you file your federal taxes using your social security number. The government has your name and number on file, and it checks out, so you are sent through the system. At the same time, however, another person uses that same social security number. He or she may also use your name, but this is not always done. The IRS flags the information for one of two reasons – either the number does not match with the name or the number has already been used on a different return. However, they still collect the tax money, as they just file the return differently because there is obviously a mistake.

Millions of returns have mistakes, after all. That is why the IRS audits people — to try to check up on returns that look strange. A weird social security number could be the result of an illegal immigrant, but it could also be a simple human error, or it could also be a computer mistake. There is no way of knowing unless there is a formal investigation, and frankly, the IRS has bigger fish to fry. At least this person (or two people using the same number) is paying taxes, and if your return is rather simple, as is the case with most immigrants who have low-paying jobs, it is easy to see that the return is correct. It is more important to the IRS to go after the people not paying their taxes at all.

That does not mean that the IRS is bad or helping illegal immigration. It just means that they have set priorities. Unfortunately for you, it means your social security number could be used for decades without your knowledge. It is not a big deal until something goes wrong. Imagine the police knocking down your door on drug charges when the person they want actually lives thousands of miles away, or if the illegal immigrant decides, after a few years, that lying low is not worth it and that opening up a fraudulent credit card or bank account makes sense. Things can go from "not so bad" to "very bad" in a matter of days.

IS IDENTITY THEFT AN ADDICTION?

I do not want suggest in any way that identity theft is excusable for any reason. That said, it can be an addiction. Some identity thieves start small, and before they know it, they are scamming people every single day. Stealing identities is a rush, and some people get addicted to that rush, the same way some people get addicted to gambling or other high-adrenaline activities. It is not always about the money. After stealing a few identities, a thief may be set financially for a few years, but that does not mean that he or she will – or can – stop.

Again, identity theft can never, ever be excused, even if the thief is a parent or the thief expresses remorse. Theft is theft. You would not excuse a bank robber for his or her crime. Just because identity theft happens online and is less personable does not mean that it is acceptable. Also, just because you are a victim that "fell" for an identity thief's scheme does not mean that it is your fault. The thief and the thief alone should take the blame.

Although the prospect that identity theft may be an addiction is, in and of itself, an interesting concept. With the right research, can we help stop identity theft by simply making sure that conditions are not right for criminal addiction to flourish? It is something researchers everywhere are interested in studying more.

The Body and Addiction

It is fairly simple to understand how the body becomes addicted to a substance such as alcohol or cocaine. When your body is used to a substance, it becomes so accustomed to the substance in question that it does not feel normal when the substance is not in the body. Our bodies then go through withdrawal, which is a lengthy time during which the body feels ill due to not having the substance. But, like I said, that is easy to understand. The harder thing to understand is how an action can be an addictive substance in the same way a drug can.

The reason an action, such as gambling or stealing identities, can be so addictive is because the body releases chemicals in the brain when we are doing these things. That "rush" you feel when you do something exciting is not just an emotion. It is also a physical reaction. You may start to sweat or your heart may begin to race, for example. If the brain gets used to these chemicals, they can have the same effects as drugs. Yes, the body contains these chemicals naturally, but you still get that "high" feeling like you would with a drug. You will not overdose and die from the excitement brought on by a risky activity, but you will still be compelled to do the activity because the body will still feel a sense of withdrawal if you stop.

Many people struggle with addiction, and are not quite sure what is going on in their brains to actually cause this obsession. The fact is that addiction is a process that is actually happening in your brain. It might feel like all of the things that are going on are actually going on in your body – but actually addiction happens in your brain.

There are several parts of addiction that happen in your brain. The first part is the actual physical addiction. This part has several functions. For instance, when a person is addicted to smoking, they are addicted in part to the actual cigarette and having it in their mouths and hands. This is something that is often overlooked, and a big part of what happens with addictions.

However, the biggest part of addictions is in the actual brain. The substance, whatever it is, that a person is addicted to, is going to cause the brain to fire differently. In the case of addiction to an activity, like crime, the "substances" are natural to the body, not like nicotine or alcohol. The elevated levels of adrenaline and other chemicals are caused by excitement act like drugs. Different substances are going to create different connections, but what happens with addiction is that the actual connections in a brain will get replaced with new connections that are all made by the drugs. These new connections actually become the way that the brain works while the person is on the drugs. What happens when the drugs are taken away is that there are major problems with recreating the connections again.

The major problem with drugs in your brain is that you will be allowing your brain to create connections that are based purely on the chemicals and not on your actual brain connections. These fake connections are going to cause many problems because your brain begins to depend on these chemical connections, instead of your actual brain connections. These fake chemicals are going to work in pretty much the same way that they work currently – except they are going to be completely fake.

Therefore, doing drugs so often so that it will replace the connections in your brain is something that will create lifelong problems with your brain. The other thing this does is send signals to the rest of your body. These are the signals that make you feel as if you need to be using the drugs. These feelings are what cause most people to actually feel as if they need the drugs. These are the feelings that are the most dangerous, because they are the feelings that are hardest to ignore. As you are not able to have the drugs, you might get even worse feelings – which will not only mess up your brain but also the way that your body works. These are all part of what happens in your brain when you do drugs.

Addiction to Crime – Inexcusable But Treatable?

There are no ifs, ands, or buts about it – crime is inexcusable, even if you are addicted to it. The real question is this – is it treatable? Treating someone is not saying, "It is OK." It is simply recognizing that there is a problem and that problem can be fixed with a little hard work.

Recognizing crime as an addiction is still relatively forward thinking. In fact, many people still question the legitimacy of such a diagnosis. How can an activity be an addiction? However, just as gambling has shown to be addictive, crime also produces chemicals in the brain for some people, creating a feeling of that "rush." Over time, the body becomes addicted to higher levels of those chemicals, which can only be obtained when committing crime. Yes, there is choice involved. At the same time, though, by getting help to the people who need it, criminals will be less tempted to commit crimes and more likely to make positive decisions.

How Can Crime Be Treated?

There are a number of tactics at play here, but one of the

most effective is the traditional twelve-step program. Made famous by Alcoholics Anonymous, this program is about taking personal responsibility for the addiction, making a real effort to overcome the addiction with the help of God, and righting wrongs. For thousands of people, the twelve-step program is extremely successful.

That said, it is not right for everyone, especially the non-religious. There are other programs that work well for criminals addicted to crime, and a number of correctional institutes run these rehabilitation programs for inmates. Sometimes, though, it is not about cracking the addiction to the "excitement" chemicals altogether – it is about finding healthy ways to achieve that same feeling to get that "fix." After all, these chemicals are natural in the body, so they are not harmful. What are some other activities that can give you that rush?

- A meaningful relationship with another person

- Extreme sports, like skydiving or mountain climbing

- Boxing or other controlled fighting

- Stock trading

- Weight training

- Jogging or other cardiovascular exercises

- Riding roller coasters and other thrilling amusement park rides

Preventing Addiction to Crime

It may sound a bit strange, but one way to fight identity theft is to prevent crime among children in general. Children are being introduced to crime at younger and younger ages, and the result is more teens and young adults are addicted to that rush they get from committing a crime. In addition, many teens and young adults turn to identity theft as a way to fund other crimes. They need money, and because they grew up around computers, they know how to scam people older than them who may not know as much about the world of the Internet.

Prevention is key. When someone is already addicted to an activity, it can be extremely hard to break that addiction, and although innovative new treatments may help, your best bet is to stop the addiction to crime before it starts. You do not have to be a parent to help. If you are a responsible adult, you can become a Big Brother or Big Sister and be a role model to a child in your community that comes from a disadvantaged family. Of course, you probably already have younger relatives that could use the help. Even if you are not particularly a fan of children, just a few hours a week can make a big difference and is not really an inconvenience to you. You might actually enjoy spending time together. Look for an activity that you already enjoy and then simply include a child you know. Getting him or her off the street for a bit can help prevent identity theft in your own backyard. Here are some activity ideas – you can surely find something on this list that sounds interesting to you:

- Go to a sports game to cheer on a local team that you both enjoy watching.

- Take a fitness class together at the local gym or recreational center.

- Attend concerts, musicals, dance recitals, or other music-related events. You may be surprised at the sophistication level of your child (or young friend).

- Go to the child's school functions. This is crucial if you are a parent, and if you are not, you may want to attend when a parent cannot. Children like to know that someone is there for support.

- Learn something new together, like how to surf or how to throw clay pots.

- Build something together. This is a good activity if you are already an accomplished woodworker and want to pass on your skills.

- Go fishing. Yes, it is cliché, but kids really do love

to get out on a boat or sit by a body of water. Cook what you catch for an extra yummy treat or make the outing into a full-fledged camping trip.

- Go shopping together. You do not have to buy anything if you have a low budget. Window shopping is fine.

AM I AT RISK?

Although the information about potential identity thieves and how your identity can be used is interesting, perhaps more important to you is learning whether are not you are at risk. The truth? Everyone is at risk for identity theft. It does not matter if you are young or old, rich or poor, or even dead. If you have an identity, it can be stolen, and there is a good chance that, sometime in your life, someone will try to steal it.

However, there are some things that put you at an even greater risk for identity theft. Check out the following points – if any of these apply to you, you are only adding to the risk of identity theft:

- You get a lot of junk mail, including several offers for pre-approved credit and debit cards every day.

- Your driver's license has your social security number printed on it.

- You use the same password for almost every online site where you are a member or have an account.

- You do not own a shredder (or you own one that you do not use).

- You are listed in a Who's Who guide.

- Any of the ID cards in your wallet that you carry all the time have your social security number printed on them.

- You have not balanced your checkbook in a long time.

- Your mailbox is not locked.

- You leave your desk at work often while you are logged into your computer.

- Your computer is not protected with a firewall or virus blocker.

- You do not follow most of the tips listed in this book.

Children at Risk

When it comes to identity theft, sometimes, unfortunately,

the people most at risk are the people who are most innocent – children. Children are at risk for a number of reasons.

First and foremost, children are at risk because parents usually do not keep their information safe. While most adults would cringe at the thought of their personal information being posted on a Web site, many parents do not bat an eyelash at posting pictures, birth dates, and other information online. While you may think that the only one who reads your personal Web site is Grandma, the truth is identity thieves everywhere will try to take advantage of the personal information you have posted online.

A child's personal information is often on record a number of places as well, making him or her an easier target. For example, schools keep records on hand to ensure that a child is getting his or her needs met, as well as to know what to do in the case of an emergency. You may have also had to provide addition personal information, like a social security number, to coaches or activities directors. To make matters worse, this information is not as highly guarded as you may think. How many secretaries does your school employ? Any one of them could have access to your child's file. Teachers and administrative personnel, as well as any support people who can smooth talk the secretaries, can get their hands on your child's information.

Children are also at risk because parents do not think to check their credit reports. Why should you check it? They do not have accounts, so nothing can be incorrect, right? Wrong. Identity thieves are banking on the fact that you probably will not check your child's credit report, meaning they can take advantage of your child's identity not just for days or weeks, but for years if they play it smart. There is some serious cash to be had with a child's identity.

Not to mention that your child still may not be following the "do not talk to strangers" rule. Sure, your three-year-old may not know her social security number to give out to a stranger, but what about your 14-year-old? If your teen is online and chatting to people on the Internet, checking his or her e-mail, etc., chances are that he or she will run into some people who are very convincing as to why they need your child's personal information. Children do not have as much life experience. Sadly, they are more easily duped.

Lastly, let us not forget that children are sometimes innocent victims to the people they trust most – their parents. It is very easy for a parent to steal his or her child's identity, using it to pay for things when their own credit is not good enough. If that is the case, it means major problems for the child when he or she turns 18, because a parent is rarely caught. You may think that your spouse would never do something like that, but it is not a matter of love. It is a matter of feeling financially trapped. Parents justify things to themselves, so you should always be sure by checking your child's credit. You never know when identity theft is going to strike.

Seniors at Risk

Many people are at risk for identity theft, yet it seems to happen more and more often to seniors. There are many reasons that seniors are more prone and more at risk to identity theft.

First of all, seniors have a lot of life experience – which also means that they have left a lot of information out there in the world. They have applied for lots of different things, and have given out their names, addresses, and social security numbers more often than people who are younger might have done. Furthermore, but it was only in recent years that lots of security measures were developed. This means many times in the past, seniors might have been giving out information to people in ways that can now be tapped, or were tapped at the time. With so much information out there, it is no wonder that lots of seniors are finding these old things coming back to haunt them.

Another reason that lots of seniors might be at risk for identity theft is that they have given their information to many businesses which might no longer exist, or which might be going out of business. When this happens, the information might not be destroyed in the right way, and this could allow a person to get the information. Due to the number of pieces of information that have been given out, it is hard to make sure that a senior is always safe.

There are other reasons that a senior might be more at risk for identity theft, in the here and now. Technology is unfortunately one of these factors. The fact remains that as technology increases, many seniors cannot keep up with it and stay behind. They might not feel it is important to learn how to use computers or the Internet, or they might learn about these things but only to an extent. Seniors are the population that has the smallest number of technology savvy people. However, they also tend to have computers, hooked up to the Internet. This makes them susceptible to fraud and identity theft because as they are using the computers for what they do know how to do, others might be stealing their information. This happens more often than seniors realize.

The final reason that seniors are more at risk for identity theft is they are the group that is least likely to pay daily attention to each of their accounts. Many of the seniors have been using the same accounts for years, and know exactly when their money will be coming. They have also not paid attention to things that have been on direct deposit or direct payment plans for years. When they have been making payments or getting payment in the same amount for many years, they might not check their bank accounts often. They are also less likely to check their bank accounts online, which means discrepancies are often not noticed until it is too late.

At Risk from Beyond the Grave

You would think that you could get some rest after you are dead and gone, right? Oddly enough, the deceased are one of the major demographics that has their identities stolen.

Identity thieves see this as an easy target. After all, how often does a dead guy check his credit history report?

Stealing from the dead is something that has been going on for quite some time. It is something that happens quite often, and they are dong it in much easier ways than you might think.

The easiest way that people steal from the dead is to find social security numbers that have belonged to dead people. This happens often because it sometimes take longer to report the deaths of people – and during the time before the deaths are reported, the numbers can be stolen and used for other things. This is something that can be devastating to lots of different people.

Another way that people steal from the dead is by stealing the social security numbers of people who have recently died. This is often done with the elderly people who might live in retirement homes. Often, the social security numbers of these people are collected, and what happens after that is a huge problem. Sometimes, when someone runs a retirement center or another place where they have access to people's social security numbers, they will take it upon themselves to steal their social security checks, which happens often. Along with stealing the checks, they will continue to receive the checks after the person has been declared dead. Sometimes, they will be able to get around the various problems with this because they will simply tell the government that the person has changed addresses, or that they have moved. Many times, people collect social security checks for many years.

Identity thieves even steal the social security numbers from people who have long since been dead. They can get these from many different sources. Often if they get them from the social security office, or if they find them from old bills and records, they will be able to use this identity for many reasons. They can take the social security numbers and create an entire identity for this person. Many times, a person will use these numbers in order to get credit cards, bank accounts, or other things from the people that they have stolen them from. This is something that you might have to take into consideration as you begin to deal with this type of identity theft.

There are many ways that criminals can steal from the dead. When this happens, there is going to be a major problem. This is because when a person has had their identity stolen, there could be a lot of money that is missing. However, when a person gets their identity stolen after they are already dead, it is going to be much harder to notice that it has happened. Many times, it will take quite a few years before relatives and others notice that money has been gone.

It works the other way around, too. If your identity is stolen, you can be reported dead when you are very much alive and well. Death also becomes a problem if your social security number has been stolen by an immigrant, who then passes away. It is already difficult to get a decent mortgage. Imagine trying to do so from beyond the grave.

Few people want to work with someone who is dead, and on paper, you very well may have kicked the bucket.

You might want to consider how you can work to save the dead from identity theft. When you have someone in your life who has died, the worst thing that you might be able to imagine is that their identity might be stolen. This is something that is actually a real fear, and it is something that happens often. When you want to protect your loved ones, you have to be sure that you are doing everything right.

It is often hard for you to protect your loved ones who have died from identity theft. However, there are some things that you can do to make sure that they are as protected as possible. You should actually begin this process if someone in your life is getting older or if they are sick. When this happens, you might be someone who is in charge of their finances or other things.

No matter what, you want to be sure that you have taken control over their finances in a way that will be useful. The first thing that you should do when you take over someone's estate – whether they have died or whether they are sick – is to make sure you have taken every chance you have to protect them. As you begin to transfer their money and take control over their accounts, you want to be sure that you are destroying all of their information that you do not need. As accounts are closed or transferred, you want to be sure that this information is not available for someone to steal.

You also want to go through all of their records and make sure that there isn't anything laying around or out in public that might be harmful. For instance, you want to be sure that you have taken all of the bank account information of someone who has died and destroyed it all. Do not simply throw it in the trash, because there is a chance that someone might find the information and use it to steal your loved one's identity. When you are dealing with the affairs of someone who has died or of someone who is incapacitated, you should make sure that you close all of their accounts. Any credit cards that they left behind should be paid off, and then closed. Any remaining cards should be cut and thrown away. All of the bank accounts and information should also be closed and destroyed. Any information that is left laying around, or any accounts or cards that are left open, will be targets for criminals and identity thieves.

When someone has died and you are in charge of their estate – or if you have access to any information about them – you want to make sure that you check their accounts and credit report often. You want to be sure that you are doing this for several years.

Risky Business: The Top Six Business Security Breaches

Every day, there are hundreds of cases of identity theft. Most days, there are thousands.

But some days, there are millions.

How are millions of identities stolen in a single day? The answer is easy – identity thefts move from targeting individuals to targeting businesses. By using computers to hack into corporations or simply by stealing sensitive documents or software, identity thieves can crack codes and steal millions of identities in a single day. Until their customers or employees begin realizing the problem and the problem is linking to the business in question, the identity thieves can continue stealing tons of identities. So, if you've ever had personal information stored in any kind of database for any reason and for any amount of time, you could be at risk. To illustrate how easily this could happen to you, let's look at the top six business security breaches in recent years. Remember, new cases are popping up every single day.

Case #1: A Bad Situation That Could Have Been Worse

In early December 2007, William Gary Sullivan admitted to stealing what he estimates as 8.5 million account records from his place of work, Fidelity National Information Services. When he found out he had access to so many identities, he set up a business front called S&S Computer Services. He then filtered the reports to his own business where he sold them to another company, who, in turn, sold them to major marketing agencies.

The subsidiary where Sullivan worked, Certegy Check Services, may have never discovered what he was doing had it not been for an intuitive business customer who noticed a correlation between certain check and junk mail. The good news here is it appears that Sullivan only sold the reports, which included names, addresses, and financial account information, to people who were interested in creating solicitation lists. The bad news is the sensitive information passed through at least four hands before making it to the end user. So far, no one has reported problems, but there very well could be instances of identity theft tied in with this case.

Bottom line? In this story, the result was bad but it could have been worse. The real problem is that oftentimes, it is worse. The people who have had their information breached in this instance can count themselves very, very lucky.

Case #2: Nigeria Gets Some Help

Teledata Communications was at the center of a huge security breach in 2005, when employee Philip Cummings, who worked at the help desk, began selling personal information to some of the people running the infamous Nigerian scams. The identity thieves hit about 300 people hard, and many more (around 30,000 people in total) had their information compromised.

Cummings' part was quite easy. Teledata Communications is a company based in New York which provides software for Equifax, Experian, and TransUnion so consumers can run credit checks. For $30 each, he sold passwords, which led the thieves to all sorts of credit information. The ring apparently made an estimated $75 million over the course of a few years by draining people's bank accounts, opening credit cards in other people's names, and convincing unknowing consumers to send money by providing accurate personal information to "prove" that this was a legitimate opportunity.

Case #3: Unsuspecting Scamming

ChoicePoint, an information colossus since 1997, was scammed by some clever criminals in 2005. These swindlers were good enough to get past the stringent security measures ChoicePoint had in place to protect their clients' information.

Through a cunning hoax perpetrated by these individuals, ChoicePoint unwittingly sold personal and financial facts of over 145,000 clients to con artists behind a nationwide identity theft plan. At least 4,500 residents in the region of the District of Columbia, Maryland, and Virginia were among those involved. Names, addresses, Social Security information, and some credit file details were included the information that is available for misuse.

ChoicePoint scrambled to try to minimize the damage and offered its clients free credit reports and free credit-monitoring services for the next year. ChoicePoint is still looking at various ways and measures to make their data more secure in the future, and lawmakers on Capitol Hill are calling for revised rules and regulations to protect people's sensitive data from this type of fraud plot in the future, citing this ChoicePoint security breach.

ChoicePoint legitimately sends its data in the form of reports to justifiable sources for the purposes of police investigations, journalism, and, ironically, fraud detection. The identity thieves who scammed ChoicePoint were posing as lawful debt collection agencies, insurance representatives, and small business personnel. They use other individual's identities and credentials to make them appear acceptable and valid in their information requests. Unfortunately, they become so knowledgeable about how to get around the system that even the experts are fooled sometimes.

Specialists in the information fields speculate this was only the beginning and that the fallout from such charlatans could reach mammoth proportions. More and more agencies rely on information collection specialists to help detect and defeat possible threats to our homeland security protection system. Federal law enforcement and intelligence officials can be helped at times by the collection of some of this data.

Several senators have asked the Federal Trade Commission to allot new rules to ChoicePoint, as rigorous as those imposed on credit reports. ChoicePoint has said they will do what it takes to ensure information is handled with the utmost care and caution to try to prevent any future recurrences. However, with identity thieves getting smarter and smarter, insiders working to help damaging cases, and many other breeches of security every year, are we really safe from another ChoicePoint-like attack? Most agree that the answer is no.

Case #4: A Clothing Store Is Hacked

Although security measures taken by many stores have been dramatically beefed up over the past few years, many are still prone to attack, as unlucky clothing retailer TJ Maxx found out in early 2007. Hackers broke into their system quite easily, accessing the credit card information for thousands if not millions of customers.

And the real problem? Once they broke into TJ Maxx's computer system, they could steal data from almost any sector of the company. TJ Maxx is just a single segment of the TJX corporation, so customers shopping at Marshalls, HomeGoods, AJ Wright, Winners, and HomeSense were also affected.

The TJ Maxx problem was due largely in part to the fact that the company runs a wireless network, as almost all do. This means you can see the network from any laptop as you're sitting outside the store. If the network's credit card system is using an outdated program, like TJ Maxx's was, you can easily look up on the Internet how to hack into that system.

Credit card companies issued directions on how to update security software over two years ago, after the first attempts at security were hacked multiple times. The newest system is, as of now, secure. However, less than half of all retailers have actually taken measures to update their systems. That means when you shop, your information is not protected over 50 percent of the time.

Have companies seen the destruction that can happen to a company that does not update its system? Has the TJ Maxx fiasco taught anyone anything? Maybe – but there are still thousands of retailers who do not protect your information, and it is impossible for you to know which ones are safe and which ones are not. Critics are calling for changes to be made so instead of the retailer holding onto your information, the credit card company does it. After all, it is easier to update a handful of systems found at the credit card companies than it is to expect millions of stores around the world to pay to update their systems every few years.

Case #5: Steps in the Wrong Direction

Although security for your data is supposed to be top of the line, many companies are continually having problems with identity thieves hacking into their systems. In June 2005, DSW (Designer Shoe Warehouse), a major shoe retailer, announced that customers who had paid by check or credit card over the last two years should put their credit reports on fraud alert. Over 1.4 million credit cards and debit cards and an additional 96,000 checking accounts were at risk after hackers made their way into the DSW system and stole information. In total, 108 locations were affected.

The good news is social security numbers were not stolen for those who shopped at these stores. However, the information that was stolen was enough to allow thieves to make online purchases and money transfers, easily draining accounts in just a few hours. Driver's license numbers were also stolen, so consumers were also recommended to call state authorities and ask if any duplicates had been created in the past few days.

Unfortunately, the most difficult part of this problem was that most of the information stolen was not connected to a number and address. While this may seem like a blessing, it was also a headache, since it meant the store could not efficiently contact all of its customers to inform them about the security breach. As a result, thousands of people lost money, some losing all of their savings to the criminals.

Case #6: Point of Sale Is a Point of Disgrace

In April 2005, there was a security breach with the Polo Ralph Lauren company. This affected people who had Discover cards, MasterCards, and Visa cards. It was a security problem that involved a point of sale system at Polo Ralph Lauren Corp.

The credit card companies that were involved notified their customers as soon as they knew about the security breach. However, it took quite some time for the companies to figure out exactly how many cardholders were affected, and how much damage was caused. In fact, this incident was so huge that it affected many, if not most, of the credit card companies in the world.

The credit card breach came up because of issues with

point of sale software. These software problems were found at a national U.S. retail chain. What happened was the credit card information that was used at this store was actually stored in this software. As the information was stored, it could then be used by other people who were trying to steal identities. What happened was that people who were working at these stores were able to gather the information and then they were able to keep the information for themselves. Later, the information was used to make other purchases, to fill out other credit card information, and to generally use identity theft in order to allow the other people to gain.

As soon as the breach was discovered, the police in the area as well as the Polo Ralph Lauren company were working together to discover who had stolen the information and where it had gone. As soon as it was discovered that the information had been kept at this point of sale retailer, the information that was found was destroyed. However, some of it had already been used in a way that was not authorized.

When the breach was discovered, HSBC bank started to send out notices to at least 180,000 of its card holders to tell them that there had been a problem, and there was a chance of potential identity thefts. This also included Visa cards, MasterCards, and Discover cards.

The security breach led to a lot of other things that happened with the credit card companies. For one, the various types of credit card companies started to check for this point of origin software. This would help them make sure that they were able to avoid this type of thing happening in the piece. It is very important that these things happened because this security breach was one of the biggest in history. When this happened, it was a huge problem for the credit card companies as well as for the people who were affected by it.

Corporate mishandling of personal information led to the loss of 70 million identities in 2006, which has generated about $1 billion in corporate losses.

3

HOW CAN MY IDENTITY BE STOLEN ONLINE?

Unfortunately, there are dozens of ways for criminals to steal your identity, and they are coming up with new scams every single day. Although the look of the scam may change, the end result is usually the same — they have received a crucial piece of information. Your first measure of protection is understanding what information can be used against you.

Right off the bat, you probably thought of your social security number. This nine-digit number is the number one thing people want to steal because, with it, they can get a job, apply for credit cards, open bank accounts, borrow money, and even use it to build credit for themselves. All this will be at the expense of your credit history. Stealing a social security number is like hitting the jackpot to identity thieves, but at the same time, it is one of the more difficult pieces of information to steal. People have long been aware of just how harmful having your social security number stolen can be, so everyone tends to protect this number closely.

Of course, there still are a number of concerns surrounding your social security number, so you should not stop protecting it. Just make sure you learn about the many other pieces of sensitive data as well. Usually, one piece of information is not enough to hurt you, but the good news for thieves is that they usually can access two or more pieces of information in a single step. Here is a list of the things you should keep private:

- **Bank Account PINs:** Your PIN is most commonly used at an ATM to draw cash from your account. A thief can steal your ATM card and, if he or she has your PIN, totally consume your money. However, even without your ATM card, a thief can make use of your PIN. By calling the bank and reporting a lost card, the thief can give your PIN and other pieces of vital information (listed below) to obtain a new card in your name.

- **Driver's License Number:** With this information, a thief can apply for a new photo identification card or even a driver's license in your name, but using his or her own picture. That comes in handy for underage teens or illegal immigrants.

- **Your Date of Birth:** Alone, it is not a big deal, but paired with other crucial information, like your social security number or your driver's license number, your date of birth will make it much easier to steal your identity.

- **Passwords:** Your passwords are crucial and most often the piece of information targeted. Using your passwords, thieves can access just about anything you have stored electronically, including your online bank accounts. Even if all they do is gain access to your e-mail account, it could ruin you financially. Using this access, they can alert other online accounts that they have "lost" their password, and the usual protocol in this case is to send account information to your preferred e-mail address. Using your e-mail address, criminals can also delete any notifications you may receive to alert you of suspicious account activity.

Other information, such as your phone number, address, mother's maiden name, and credit card number can all contribute to the theft of your identity. Although this information can be found no matter how hard you try to protect it, use some common sense. If someone is going to try to steal your information, do not make it easy.

There are few times when you should give that sort of information out, but it is important to note here that there is one time to do it – when the police or government is involved. Although you should resist giving out personal information, if you are 100 percent sure that the person asking for the information is a police officer or government official, give it out or you could face criminal charges.

Be aware, however, that you have rights to protect yourself. Most people know, for example, that if they see flashing red lights and are on a deserted stretch of road, they are well within their rights to put on their four-ways and drive to the nearest shopping center or other lit area. It is simply protection; you want to make sure that the person pulling you over is really a cop, not a carjacker that bought a flashing police light off of eBay. It is the same when someone "official" asks for your information. You are well within your rights to wait until you are really at the government office (police station, city hall, etc.) to give out that information – as long as you state that respectfully. Make sure that you are only giving your personal information to people who have been given the authority to securely handle it.

HACKING

Computer hacking is one of the ugliest, most mean-spirited white-collar crimes. Hacking sometimes focuses on stealing identities, but other times, it just seeks to destroy people's computers and information in order to gain notoriety and a reputation in the online world. In other words, some hackers create viruses simply to create problems. Due to that, some people believe that hacking is not really a problem when it comes to identity theft. If that is your mindset, you are one of the people most at risk.

Symantec Corp., one of the world's largest anti-virus program producers, found that the trends in hacking have begun to move from notoriety crimes to theft crimes; while once only accounting for 20 to 25 percent of all hacking crimes, identity theft is now the main focus of an astounding 75 percent or more of all hackers. As hackers begin to find out how profitable stealing information can be, this trend will only continue. Even the programs just created to cause problems can be a potential threat to your identity. When a virus attacks your computer, it creates all kinds of security problems, making you an easier target for other criminals.

The sad thing about the hacking situation is many hackers are trained to actually help the computer world. Companies employ hackers to help create programs, test the air-tightness of specific concepts, and remedy situations in which passwords and usernames are lost or misused. Hacking in and of itself is valuable, not a crime — it is the use of a skill that creates a threat to the general public. Stopping hackers can be extremely difficult, but your first step in this battle is learning about the many different ways hackers can attack you.

Bots

Anyone who knows anything about computer programming can make a simplified version of a bot. A really good programmer can make really good bots. Even if you are not a programmer at all, you can still use a bot. People have them for sale all the time, and bots are not just annoying.

They can be used to steal your identity.

People created bots to do many things. Some of them can search the Internet for e-mail addresses that are on Web sites and are not protected. Some of them will send various spam messages to people. Bots can also get onto forums and sign up on them – where they can access your personal information such as your passwords and other things. All in all, bots were created to be a program that could go online as if it were a real person (or people), and gather as much information as possible.

Bots are dangerous because they search for information at lightening speeds. This can include addresses, phone numbers, e-mail addresses, and even things that you might not think are important – but are – such as birthdays that can be used in identity theft. The bots are worse than a person collecting this information however – because the bots are much smarter than a person and are also able to go to thousands of Web sites, 24 hours a day. These bots can work constantly to gather information, and they never need to stop. They can travel from Web site to Web site constantly gather information. Then, all of the information is sent to whoever owns the bot.

The other reason that bots are so harmful is they are also able to put information together in a much smarter way than a person could. They can look at your IP address and figure out which of the information is yours. They can also gather things that you might consider to be hidden online. Therefore, bots are very, very dangerous.

As you are protecting yourself from bots, the best way to do this is to make sure that you are able to avoid putting any information online whatsoever. Remember that bots can collect any type of information from your online sites – even parts of information that you might think are hidden. Therefore, the best thing that you can do is to protect yourself by making sure that you are able to keep as much of your own personal information off the Internet as you can.

Account Hacking and Backdoors

Backdoors are built into almost every computer program, and while they can be very helpful if you forget your password or otherwise have a problem, they are also often targets for scammers. You do not even have to be a knowledgeable hacker to gain access through a program's backdoor. You just have to be a smooth talker.

Imagine that you have an account, for example, through your business for an anti-virus program. You use it without trouble for a few months, go on vacation, and then return home and head back to work. In your absence, however, you have completely forgotten your password. There is no built-in way to e-mail the password to yourself, so you call the company, hoping they can help you regain access.

And they probably can. Companies assume that people just like you are going to forget their passwords, so they build in systems to work around that login information. These are called backdoors. While a good backdoor can save you a lot of time, the problem with backdoors is they make any computer program much less secure. Anyone with backdoor access can potentially find a way to steal your identity.

Hacking happens more easily than you may think as well. Basically, hacking is when someone who is not supposed to have access to your account finds a way to get into your account anyway, many times through cracking your code – i.e., figuring out your password. There are a number of ways hackers can figure out your password for any given Web site or login program:

- **The Dictionary Attack:** Hackers have created programs that run based on dictionary words. These programs attempt to log in using every word in the dictionary. Since most people use a very simple password, this cracks a high percentage of passwords wide open. Hackers do not even have to really work in order to guess your password with this method. They simply set up the program to run and wait a few hours until a positive match is found.

- **The Hybrid Attack:** Like the dictionary attack, hackers do not have to do much work to figure out your password with a hybrid attack. These programs run the same way, but use numbers and special characters as well. Many people use a simple word, like "computer" and then, to attempt to make it more secure, they add on a number to make their password something like "computer2". The more sophisticated hybrid programs most hackers use check for number add-ons like this.

There are a number of other ways hackers can get into your account as well. It is important to remember, however, that the label "hacker" is not necessarily a bad thing. Yes, there are good hackers, as weird as that may sound. Although the media often uses the term hacker to purely mean someone who attacks your account or a computer program, "good" hackers are employed by all major software companies in order to find program weaknesses. Hackers help make your information more secure! Here is a run-down of hacker classification:

- White hat hackers: Anyone termed a "white hat" hacker is someone who is working with the company to find security weaknesses, working with the government to catch criminals, and so forth.

- Gray hat hackers: Gray hat hackers are those who fall into gray area. They use their hacking skills for morally and ethically ambiguous matters and often toe the line of legality.

- Blue hat hackers: These hackers are not company employees, but help to test a program before launch. They are like freelance white hat hackers. The work they are doing is usually good, although since they are not responsible to the company in terms of being an employee, the temptation to exploit what they've found is much greater.

- Black hat hackers: Black hats are the "bad guys," although they do not always see themselves as such. It is a black hat hacker that will try to steal your identity using hacking techniques. Of course, some black hat hackers, like some criminals, believe that what they are doing is for the greater good, so not every black hat hacker is trying to steal your identity.

When talking about hackers, you may also hear the term "script kiddie." This is a hacker who does not have much skill or experience with hacking. Script kiddies usually simply follow directions from more experienced hackers, which you can find on the Internet. They do not know what they are doing or why they are doing it – they just know that the steps work. Many identity thieves are nothing more than script kiddies. They frequent hacker forums and message boards and look for ways they can use the ideas posted to steal identities from others. That is why an excellent password will stop most identity thieves in their tracks – when they hit a bump in the road, they do not have the knowledge to figure out what to do next.

SPYWARE

A study done by a security firm in 2006 found that 40 percent of all spyware programs are meant to be used for stealing personal data and an additional 30 percent are meant to be used for other illegal purposes. That means 70 percent of all spyware programs are designed for identity crimes. An even scarier stat? Webroot took a survey of over a million computers and found that 88 percent had spyware installed on a personal computer and 87 percent had spyware installed on a business computer.

Spyware is made up of various programs that can get downloaded onto your computer. Often this happens in ways that might not be your fault. You might find that spyware is on your computer and you really have no idea how it got there or where it came from. This is because there are many forms of spyware that come attached to other programs. You might think that you are downloading something that is perfectly innocent – but it might contain a hidden piece of spyware that you weren't even aware of. When this happens, you will find that you have to deal with these issues.

Spyware works in a variety of ways, and all of these ways might create a situation where your identity is at risk. Spyware is a type of program that you are always going to be having run on your computer. Most of it will be able to run on its own, which means you won't even have to click on the program to start it. Often, the only way that you will know the spyware is there is to check in your add and delete programs files in order to see it. Some of the spyware might not even show up here, and you might need extra programs in order to even find it.

The reason that spyware is going to be so detrimental to your computer and to your identity is that the purpose of the spyware is to collect information. Sometimes, the spyware is created to show the owners of the spyware where people are going online. This can then be used to form advertising that is more guaranteed to be something that you will follow through with. Most of the spyware on the market started like this – so that advertising could be targeted and allow you to get even more out of it. However, it quickly accelerated. Part of the reason that spyware is now so dangerous is along with collection information about where you are going online, they are also used to collect your personal information. As your personal information is collected by the spyware, it can be stored somewhere that people might have access to that data. This is something that you want to think carefully about, because as you are doing your dealings online you might find that someone has gotten much more than your online history out of it. They might actually be able to see where you have been online and what you have been doing. These cases can be very dangerous to you, because if you are online often, you might find that there are many situations where you end up with your identity stolen.

An example of spyware that might help an identity thief steal your identity is one that records keystrokes. Let's say, for example, that you download a music file from someone on a Web site message board. However, you were unaware that the file had a little bonus present – a spyware program attached to it. You download and open the music file and immediately the keystroke spyware begins running on your computer as well. The identity thief then sees any key you press. How does that help the identity thief? Well, say he or she sees that you hit the keys w – w – w - . – y – a – h – o – o - . – c – o – m – enter. Then he sees you hit t - . – s – m – i – t – h – 9 – 8 (common keystrokes for a username). He knows you are signing into your e-mail. Whatever keys you hit next are the keys to your password. This can be even more dangerous if the identity thief sees that you have signed into a banking Web site.

This form of spyware is not the only kind you have to worry about. There are many kinds of spyware and all are equally damaging to your computer. In short, beware of spyware. It can ruin your life.

SPAM

In 2004, 65 percent of all e-mails sent over the Internet were spam — junk, unsolicited, bulk messages. Many people avoid both spam and phishing because they do not want to fall victims to identity theft. However, spam is more detrimental than you might think. Phishing is easy to fall for, but once a person recognizes it, it is also easy to avoid. Spam can be a bit harder to avoid.

Spam is easier to fall for because a lot of it seems like it might actually be a good idea. This is part of why people fall for it so often – it simply seems like they will be able to get something for nothing, or to buy a great product. Part of the problem with spam is it is everywhere, and also that it is very hard to trace. As the products are offered, your identity can be stolen.

Spam is what comes into your inbox that can promise you all kinds of great products. These might be anything from enhancements for your body, to toys or games, to books or property. Spam makers and sellers can offer you just about anything for sale, and it usually seems like it will be a good deal. It also might seem very legit. There are many people who want to have the products that are being sold, so they'll pay for it. A more dangerous method of spam is actually offering free items. A person would love to get something for free, so by offering free items, it is easier to get people to agree.

Whether they have convinced someone to buy something, or to get a free item, the identity thief will then ask for information. Of course, if you agree to purchase something, you will have to provide your credit card number to purchase your item. Once you have given it to the identity theft, he or she will be able to use the credit card. There are also other dangers that go along with spam. In order to buy something you will have to provide your card, the other numbers that go on it, your full name, and billing and shipping address. This is almost all of your personal information, and if you provide this to someone who is not actually selling a product, you have given your number to a thief.

There are other ways that identity thieves can get you through spam. Even when they offer you something for free, they will often ask you for your credit card information – often to prove that you are a real person, or to prove where you live – or even so that you might make additional purchases from them. No matter what their reason might be for getting your credit information, you probably will not get that free product, and you might end up owing a lot more in the long run.

Secure sites are the only safe way to purchase things online. Buying things that come into your spam box or even into your inbox can be extremely dangerous for you. Do not be fooled, no matter how great the deal might seem to be.

PHISHING AND SPOOFING

Spoofing is one of the easiest ways to steal someone's identity. Millions of people have responded to spoofed e-mails and Web sites, meaning that this is an online cash cow for crooks. Sadly, as online banking and having other online accounts gets more and more popular, spoofing gets easier and easier. The problem is most people have no idea this scam is even happening. Spoofing has two main forms: e-mail and Web site.

E-mail Spoofing (Phishing)

If there were a problem with your account, you would expect the financial institution to contact you by phone, e-mail, and snail mail as soon as it is discovered. You would want to take action as quickly as possible, and you would want to make sure that you were as thorough as you could be in stopping the threat. From suspicious activity to password problems to security threats, getting any kind of correspondence that indicates a problem with your account is enough to send anyone into panic mode. In fact, that is exactly what spoofing scammers are counting on to happen.

E-mail spoofing, also called phishing, is one of the fastest growing crimes on the Web. A study done by the Anti-Phishing Working Group found that 5 percent of the 75 to 150 million phishing e-mails sent every day are actually answered. That is a very high rate of return for scammers, making phishing one of the most popular ways to steal your identity online.

Here is the basic concept: First, the scammers collect a list of people with accounts at a particular financial institution. This might be information from a bank, a credit card company, or even an online auction site. Almost any financial account could be at risk. The only thing the thief needs to get started is your name and e-mail address. Depending on the complexity of the scam, the thief can work from there or he or she can spend extra time looking up your birthday, address, or other personal information, most of which can easily be found through public records on the Internet.

The thief may also take the extra step to copy the financial institution's look and feel. This can be done through links back to the institution's Web site, use of a masthead, use of legitimate officer names, and so forth. It depends on how much time the scammer is willing to take to be successful. When it is all said and done, the thief will send you an e-mail, saying that there was a problem with your account. The problem varies from scam to scam, and the thief may even relay "personal" information, like your birthday, back to you to "prove" that it is a legitimate e-mail. The e-mail will then ask you to do one or two things — call a number for account verification or reply to the e-mail for account verification. In either case, the scammer will likely ask for your password so that it can be reset to deter the person trying to break into your account. If a thief is really feeling lucky, he or she will also ask for your social security number to verify that you are, in fact, the owner of the account.

It might be days or even weeks until you start seeing the effects of this scam, depending on what information was stolen. There was never any problem with your account; the scammer just wanted you to release personal information.

Remember that your financial accounts are not the only things at risk. Any online account you have is at risk, including ones that you do not think mean anything, like a subscription to an online magazine or a social networking account. Phishers will use every opportunity to find out information about you. Say, for example, the con artist contacted you through MySpace, a popular networking site. You are told that your account is in danger of deletion unless you verify your user name, real name, and password. Your password will then be reset, you are told, and you can pick a security question to prevent this from happening again. Your MySpace account is simply pictures and song lyrics, so even though it is annoying to have another person sign into it and pretend to be you, does it really matter? Absolutely. The criminal is probably banking on the fact that you have other online accounts that you use the same password for or a similar version. Your security question answer ("Who was your favorite teacher in high school?" or "What was your first pet's name?") is also probably the security question you use in other places. You are giving the scammer access to other places, unless you are one of the few people who actually use different random passwords with every account. Most people do not, which is how e-mail spoofing thrives.

IP Address Spoofing

You can also be attacked by IP (Internet Protocol) spoofers. This is a much more sophisticated kind of e-mail spoofing attack and can really wreak havoc on you and your personal information. Whenever you send anything over the Internet, which is usually (but not always) done via e-mail, there is a personal IP address attached to it. Let's take a non–e-mail example: Say you are reading a blog and want to leave a comment for the author about a particular post. When you hit "submit" and post your comment, your IP address is attached to that comment. Your IP address is unique to your computer and allows the person receiving the data (in this case, the comment sent to the blogger on a Web site) to see where the comment is coming from. In the case of blogging, this is important because a person can block harassing users or track statistics from certain areas. You IP address, which is just a series of numbers is also attached to e-mails, downloaded and uploaded information, and just about any interaction on the Internet.

Although it is usually hidden, a scammer with some computer Internet know-how can see that IP address in the header of whatever he or she is sending before it is sent. That way, they can go in and change that information, which from a technical standpoint makes the data look like it is coming from a completely different source altogether. Why would anyone do this?

Well, in most cases, the scammer simply wants to create problems within a system so that legitimate e-mails are deleted along with legitimate e-mails. The network is so overwhelmed with fake e-mails that it has to shut down completely to handle the attack. This can also prevent legitimate people fro accessing sites. Say, for instance, scammer attacks a bank with money requests. Getting hundreds of fake money requests every minute, all from spoofed IP addresses, can make it impossible to sort out the real money requests.

Most of the time, this just causes trouble and delays. The scammer has nothing to gain, in a monetary sense at least. However, IP spoofing can be really dangerous on a network, like you'd find at work. If the hacker can intercept e-mails and change the IP address to reroute everything to his or her own computer, sensitive information can be sent to the wrong person, putting identities at risk. This is one of the main reasons why it is very, very important to use password protection methods when setting up a wireless router in your own home. Otherwise, anyone sitting outside your door can potentially get into your system and cause trouble rerouting e-mails.

Web Site Spoofing

Even more dangerous than phishing (e-mail spoofing attacks) is Web site spoofing. This is a complex skill to acquire, but not hard to pull off once you learn how to do it. As with e-mail spoofing, the level of complexity is determined by the amount of time a criminal puts into planning the attack. While amateurs can set up this kind of scam in about a day (or even less), others may go to great lengths to cover all their bases. When someone wants to scam you to steal your identity, they will spend the time it takes to do it right. After all, the payoff is huge. If they get your credit card number, it could mean thousands in profit. Multiply that dollar amount by hundreds or even thousands, depending on how many people fall for their scam. They are willing to spend a few weeks or even months creating an airtight scheme.

The most amateur way to go about spoofing a Web site is simply to copy its look and feel. Take PayPal, for example. This Web site is commonly used to send and receive money, and if anyone accesses your account, they can transfer all the money in said account to their own bank account or another PayPal account. Using a computer photo editing program or Web site building program, a scammer can take the homepage of PayPal and recreate it exactly but post it at another Web address. This scammer is banking on the fact that you will not notice that a link redirects you to a site other than paypal.com. You will see the sign in box, but instead of signing in, the site will simply record your e-mail and send it to the thief's e-mail address. You will see a screen pop up that says you have entered the password incorrectly, and you will be redirected to the real PayPal site to try again. This time it will work, and you will probably never think twice about the first error — after all, we all make typos now and again. In a few hours, your PayPal account will be looted.

Of course, the best thing about this scam for you is the thieves do not invest much time or money into it, so you should be able to notice the weird Web address. In any case, someone will notice (usually relatively quickly) and notify PayPal. In a matter of a few days or even hours, the fraudulent site will be shut down, hopefully catching the criminal before he or she disappears, although you cannot rely on that. In any case, the less thought out, the better.

It is not always easy, unfortunately. Any seasoned identity thief will realize that it is worth the extra time to think the plan through instead of getting shut down and facing criminal charges in a matter of hours after only stealing a few passwords. Instead, they use an even trickier spoofing technique. They start the same way — by creating a Web site with the same look and feel of the original. However, instead of buying a random domain name and hoping that you do not notice, they will go that extra mile and buy an international domain name (IDN). IDNs are causing a lot of trouble around the world.

If you are not interested in the domain name buying and selling industry, IDNs can be a hard concept to understand, so do not be alarmed if it takes some time to wrap your head around the idea. Let us start simply by talking about languages. In every language, you will have a slightly different alphabet. Think about French, for example, from which we get the word résumé. Because this word is so integral to the English language, we often write it "resume" without the special characters, but the "é" in résumé is not the same as the "e" in any other word in this sentence. It has to do with an alphabet that is different from English. Even though a Web site's standard is to be written in English, this is not always the case.

In fact, when you go to different countries, there are different keyboards. These help to accommodate all the other letters that we do not have. Cyrillic, a language of the Middle East, is one of the biggest culprits in IDNs because they have quite a number of "special" letters. However, like with resume and résumé, when you handwrite the letters, they are often very similar. Typing them on an English keyboard then becomes a problem. The website resume.com is not the same as the Web site résumé.com — although both Webmasters might advertise it as resume.com. I know — it is difficult to follow. That is what makes this scam so great — most people do not understand it.

Resume.com might not be a huge threat, but think about our PayPal example before. In other languages, the letter "â" is used. Imagine, then, what happens if someone registers the domain name pâypal.com or even goes a step further and replaces both "a"'s with the wrong letter. They own **paypal.com**, but not the paypal.com that you think you will see when you use the site. This causes a lot of confusion. In the past, PayPal actually was the victim of such a spoofing attack, and thousands of users' passwords were stolen.

An easier way to spoof Web sites is to use English letters that look similar. Pretend for a moment that you have an account with **1stCreditBank.com**. What happens if someone buys that same domain name with a lower-case "L" as the first character instead of a number one? Side by side, 1 and l look exactly the same. Zeros, capital I's, and a number of other English keyboard characters also look alike. The font matters, too. In one font, two characters may look completely different, but in another font, they may be very similar. Identity thieves will play with fonts until they find one that works well for their scheme. It is your responsibility to play with fonts until you catch them. It is fairly easy to dupe a victim if you try, and the only way to notice that the site you are clicking is not a fake site is to be observant. IDNs will translate different once you have clicked on the link, for example. You can easily recognize an IDN by the first two characters — xn.

Once you are at the site, the process is the same. You will be asked to sign-in, and the login will redirect you to the real site while simultaneously sending an e-mail with your information to the site's owner.

Some criminals even use their spoofed Web sites in conjunction with a phishing e-mail. They may send you a short note saying that your account may have been compromised and that you should log in to review your transaction history. The e-mail will include a handy link to the site where you have the account. This link will take you to the fake site. So, the crimes continue to multiply, and as soon as one scammer is caught, ten more pop out of the woodwork.

COMMON SCAMS

Within each of the scamming categories, there are dozens of specific scams that people use to steal identities. In this section, some of the most common scams are listed. However, keep in mind that identity thieves will always come up with new stories. It is kind of like a child giving a teacher excuses as to why he or she did not do any homework. That old "the dog ate it" will not work anymore, so children are becoming more resourceful. Some of the same excuses prevail – "I forgot my books" or "I didn't understand how to do it" – but new excuses evolve with time. Today's children might say, "My computer crashed," for example. By this time next year, there will be even more excuses made popular by lazy tykes everywhere.

Teachers are smart, and you should be smart about identity theft. New scams will pop up every day, so stay in tune with popular trends. These old, classic types of scams listed here will still circulate from time to time, but do not look at this list at all as exhaustive. The more information you have about popular scams, the better you can avoid them.

Mortgage Scams

In the United States, mortgage fraud rose almost 400 percent from 2002 to 2005. Some of the hotspots for this fraud include Georgia, South Carolina, Florida, Michigan, Illinois, Missouri, California, Nevada, Utah, and Colorado.

The most common type of mortgage scam occurs not online, but rather in face-to-face interactions with dishonest lenders. The contract that you sign is different than what you have been led to expect. Lenders can pull this off in a number of ways:

- The lender may talk about one thing but the contract may say another. They get away with this because few people read the contract all of the way through, worrying that they are taking too much time to do so or somehow offending the lender because they are showing that they do not "trust" that the contract is fair. If caught, the lender may act surprised, like it is a mistake, and will quickly fix the contract. However, if you sign the contract and it is not what you were led to believe, you are, in many times, simply out of luck. There is no way to prove that a certain conversation happened. The contract is supposed to reflect the verbal conversation.

- The lender may leave things blank where they can be filled in. Is there a certain number filled in for the interest rate, for example? If not, after you sign it, the lender can fill in whatever number he or she wants to fill in, which may be much higher than you actually verbally agreed.

- After you read the mortgage agreement, but before you sign it, the lender replaces it with a fresh version for some reason. Maybe you spotted a typo. Maybe he or she spilled coffee on it. Whatever the problem, if the agreement is out of your sight any time after you read it, read it again before you sign it. Some of the information may have been magically changed.

- The wording could be purposely confusing. If you do not understand something on your contract, you are likely to pass it by, trying to look like you understand everything. Many people get pulled into balloon schemes in this process. A balloon loan is when you have very low payments and a very low interest rate for the first year or two, and then suddenly the entire loan comes due. If you cannot repay it in full, you are forced to refinance, often for very high fees and a very high interest rate.

You can also be scammed when taking out a mortgage if you use a lender that is not really a lender. This person will simply take your personal information in order to "check your credit history." However, in reality, you will never be approved – there is no money. He or she is not really a lender – that company is just a front used to steal your personal information. Never give away your information to a lender unless you first check to be sure that he or she is legitimate.

This is especially common online, where new lenders seem to pop up every day. Remember, these so-called lenders can say whatever they want to on their sites, including making up fake testimonials. Before you trust anyone with your information, make sure that you do a thorough investigation. Check with the Better Business Bureau, call phone numbers to make sure that they are legitimate, and further take measures to ensure that the lender really is a lender, not someone simply collecting personal information.

Auction Scams

Auction scams are all too common. Studies show that 40 percent of all auction buyers have had problems with their transactions. Considering some 35 million Americans have participated in online auctions that means 14 million people have had problems, accounting for 75 percent of all complaints with the Internet Crime Complaint Center.

The scary thing about online auctions is the unknown. On most sites, it is very easy to sign up for an account, and you can use a fake name and address if you want. If there is a problem, it is your word against the seller's word. It is hard to prove that the transaction did not go as planned. Unless you use a reputable escrow service, you will probably have to resort to leaving a bad rating and counting your losses. There is not much else you can do to ensure that the fraudulent seller is brought to justice.

There are a number of ways in which you can be scammed on online auction sites:

- You might never receive the item after paying for it. It is always "in the mail."

- The item might be broken or drastically different than what you thought you were buying. Be careful to read the description, however, since many items are sold in non-working condition or come with disclaimers that the actual item may be a bit different from the pictured item.

- Your credit card number could be stolen, leading to complete identity theft.

- The escrow service the seller wants to use could be fake, meaning that you have lost the money and sensitive information.

- Someone could hack into your account and use it to bid on items or sign up as a seller and scam other people. They also can often find sensitive information, like your e-mail address and password, in your account.

The problem with online auction scams is they are extremely hard to fight. If you get scammed in an online auction and try to seek legal action, nine times out of ten, you will be throwing good money after bad money. That does not mean that you should not try to bring the bad guys to justice. You should! Just be aware going into an auction that nine out of ten people are too trusting and do not ask for contact information, escrow services, or contracts. Protect yourself, especially if the auction item is fairly expensive.

The main threat here is actually not the loss of your money, but the loss of your identity. While paying for an item that you never receive can be a blow to your budget, paying for an item and then having your credit card number stolen is much, much worse. On top of that, if you entered other personal information, like your social security or driver's license number as "confirmation" (like many escrow services ask that you do), the thief who started that fake escrow service now has enough information to get a job in your name, open credit card accounts, take out loans at the bank, and even use your identity to run from the law. It is a scary situation.

Online Dating Scams

There are multiple varieties of online dating scams, and these are often the most tragic of all online scams. With online dating scams, it is not just your identity that is attack; it is also your heart on the line. Online dating is becoming more and more popular every day, and so online dating scams are on the rise. No one is suggesting that you avoid online dating altogether, as many people really are finding true, legitimate love online. Protection is the key.

Online dating scams started long before eHarmony and Match ever existed. Mail order brides and the companies that represented them were the first of the online dating scammers, and actually, mail order brides existed even before the Internet. Usually "selling" brides from Eastern Europe or Asia, mail order bride companies try to steal your identity in two main ways.

First, there may not even be any brides, and the company itself could be scamming you. Beware of any mail order bride company that contacts you via e-mail. A legitimate company will advertise, but allow you to come to them. Keep in mind, however, that any mail order company might scam you. Sometimes, there are not brides at all. With this type of scam, the company may show you pictures or even send you fake letters and e-mails from potential brides. This may go on for weeks or months, but once you choose a bride to sponsor and send in the payment for a visa (or whatever they say they need the money for) the company – and your bride – will disappear. It is especially easy to spot these companies in some cases because they use a PO Box mailing address and are not registered with their state. They also often will not know how to answer your immigration questions, which a legitimate company should be able to do. Do some digging by asking questions, and if they are avoided or answered incorrectly, you know there is a problem.

Sometimes, the company is legitimate, and it is the girl who is scamming you. Yes, mail order bride companies do legitimately exist, and although many people have moral issues with this kind of business, they really can help bachelors find brides in some cases. Just make sure that your bride really wants to be with you. Many of these girls simply want to get to the United States and will lie to find a meal ticket and sponsor. So how can you tell?

Unfortunately, you often cannot tell the difference. Communication online does not make it easy to catch a liar, and even telephone conversations may not alert you to the fact that the girl does not really care about you. Face to face meetings are crucial, but even before that, keep your guard raised. Do not fall in love too quickly with anyone who has so much to gain from loving you. That advice stands true not just with mail order brides. This is the shadowy side of people dating online – are they trying to use you and possibly attempting to steal your identity?

Do not fall into the trap that this online dating scam cannot happen to you because it can. It happens to smart people every day. Emotions have a funny way of affecting your judgment, making it easy for scammers to take advantage of you. In fact, this is exactly what scammers are hoping will happen. The lies one person tells will differ greatly from the lies another person will tell, simply because it only depends on the scammer's creativity.

Basically, the scammer wants you to fall in love. After all, you will do anything for the person you love, right? That includes sending money, having physical relationships, buying gifts, and giving up personal information. These scammers want you to trust them so much that, even after you feel like you have been scammed, you do not believe it's possible. Many victims never alert the police because they do not comprehend what happened or they are too embarrassed to admit that they fell in love with someone who scammed them. If no one goes to the police, the scammer can simply start over again with little worry, which is the main draw of this kind of sweetheart scam. Online dating scams take a lot more time than many of the other scams on this list, but the payout is great. Plus, although this sounds horrible, dating scams are more "fun." Would you rather try cracking passwords all day or talk online to someone falling in love with you?

Online dating scams start with an initial meeting. Mail order brides are just the beginning. You will also find scammers in chat rooms, on instant messenger programs like Yahoo! Messenger or AIM, on forum message boards, on social networking sites like Facebook or MySpace, and even on the one site where you should be safe – the online dating site. Online dating sites are made to help you find love, so of course, users want to believe that everyone on the site is there for the same reason. Unfortunately, these sites are playgrounds for scammers. That is not to say that you cannot find a legitimate relationship online, because you can. However, you have to be very, very careful. Online dating is risky and your identity could be quickly put in harm's way.

After the initial contact, you will probably find that most scammers will push the relationship forward fairly quickly. They will say that they feel a connection and may even say that they love you rather quickly. Of course, this might happen in a real relationship as well, so it cannot be the deciding factor as to whether or not the man or woman is a scammer, but it is a good indication.

On top of quickly "falling for you," a warning signal of a possible online dating scam is the unavailability of information. The scammer will be much more interested in your life than willing to talk about him- or herself. Scammers often do not lead the life they say they lead because they want to be hard to catch. For example, a scammer will typically lie about his or her job, family, education, and so forth. The key to noticing the scam is to look for inconsistencies in the stories. Most scammers use a single story as they move from victim to victim, but the story does have to change slightly. Otherwise, the community online would rally to catch the scammer. Typically, small changes in the story make the scammer's victims less likely to meet up with one another. The scammer may also change his or her story to better draw you in. For example, if you share that you have recently lost a parent, he or she may talk about the death of a loved one to find that heart-wrenching connection.

Playing games in a relationship, on or offline, is never a good idea. That said, you should attempt to look for inconsistencies in an online friend's story. If the scammer feels like things are beginning to fall apart, he or she will leave or start to ask for money and/or information from you, and believe me: an online dating scammer will have no mercy. It is important to remember that anyone who can say "I love you" online before meeting or even talking to you in person, face to face, probably does not mean it.

If you feel that strongly, set up a safe in-person meeting to truly explore your feelings with the other person.

However, many people do "fall in love" online, and when that happens, the scammer will begin to look for opportunities to steal your identity. He or she may ask for money, plane tickets to come see you, help co-signing for a car, and so forth. There will always be good reasoning behind why the scammer needs you to help. Deaths in the family are common, for example. And who would not help someone they love with a few hundred dollars to pay for a funeral?

Scarier than losing money, though, is losing your identity. There is absolutely no reason that an online relationship partner should need your social security number, credit card number, driver's license number, or other personal information. None. Often, at this point, he or she will pull the "But if you loved me..." card if you seem at all hesitant. In reality, a person who loves you will not ask for these things in the first place.

Know the law, especially if your online sweetheart resides in another country. Certain documents and personal information may actually be needed to allow immigration, but there is no need for you to give out that information to your partner. Instead, work only with government officials. Do not be afraid to do a little snooping, finding out as much as you can about anyone you meet online before you attempt any kind of relationship.

There is one other main way you can be the victim of an

online dating scam. If someone steals your password, he or she can pretend to be you in order to get a date. This is most common if you have a desirable profile with lots of great pictures. Sometimes, jealous family members or ex-girlfriends or boyfriends also try to log in to pretend to be you. Identity theft does not always mean that the other person is trying to steal your money. Someone who uses your identity for online dating is doing other kinds of damage. It is still a serious matter.

Pharmaceutical Scams

Millions of drug scam e-mails go out every day, and a study in 2004 actually found that pharmaceuticals were the most common topic of e-mail scams on the Internet — they even overtook porn as a scam leader. Pharmaceutical scams are popular, but they are also hard to stop simply because every country has different laws regarding what kinds of drugs can and cannot be sold online. Proving that a real crime is happening is harder than just shutting down a Web site. Most sites cannot be shut down purely for selling drugs. The way to nail these scammers is to prove that they are selling drugs that are not what they say they are or to prove that they are using the pharmaceutical shop as a storefront for an identity theft scheme. Those two things can be hard to prove.

It may seem easy – simply have an undercover agent attempt to purchase drugs and then see what happens. The problem lies in the fact that these companies are here one day and gone the next. They use private registration to purchase a Web site or, worse, use the credit card information of someone they have scammed to buy a domain name. They use dishonest means to find your e-mail address and then send out spam e-mail as fast as possible. Even if only 1 percent of all people who receive e-mails reply, that is still a pretty fair number considering that they send out millions of e-mails.

But what is the harm? We can just delete the e-mails and move on, right? An Internet-savvy person will do just that, but for some people who are not as experienced, pharmaceutical Web sites seem like a fairly easy way to purchase the drugs they need for a cheaper price. After all, prescriptions and doctor's appointments can be expensive. Pharmaceutical sites capitalize on the fact that not everyone in the United States has health insurance. In fact, a good percentage of people do not. These same people are less likely to be educated about identity theft online. Therefore, they log on and attempt to order drugs online. Sometimes they get them; sometimes the pills are perpetually in the mail.

There are three main ways a pharmacy scam can run. Note that not all online drug sites are trying to scam you. A few are legitimate, but you should always proceed with caution, as a good majority is not valid. They all have one thing in common, however. They want your money.

First, an online drug site could actually be selling the drugs they advertise. Note that this is rare unless the site really is legitimate. However, it does happen. Someone has access to prescription drugs, so they sell them online for a cheap price. They do not want a doctor's official prescription; they just want your money. Consider this kind of site illegal, although it does depend on where you live. In any case, ordering here is a crapshoot. It is like buying something at an online auction. You cannot be sure as to how trustworthy the seller is, so he or she may take of your payment and "forget" to mail out what you have ordered.

The second and third types of online drugstore are a bit more complicated and you have a lot more at risk. They will not, however, look any different than the one that really will send out your prescription, which is why this process can be so confusing. The second type is scamming you for your money, but not in a way that you will realize in a long time. They are not sending you the real thing. Their pills are filled with "filler" substances that make the prescription useless. You might as well be eating candy instead. In some cases, the pills are composed of the correct ingredients, but in the wrong ratios. They may be stronger or weaker than the real version of the pill or they may cause strange side effects. In any case, this is not only unhealthy, but could be downright dangerous. You never know what is going to be in your prescription drugs if you do not get them from a reputable source, like your local neighborhood pharmacy with a doctor's prescription.

The third major way in which online drug companies can scam you is by actually stealing your information. They may say that they need your social security number for confirmation, or they may take your credit card information and use it to ring up fraudulent charges. They want to gather as much information about you as possible because the more information a thief has, the more money he or she can make from you. Identity thieves want to make as much money as possible, so they will push you to share all kinds of personal information. Since so many people want or need pharmaceutical services, it is easy to scam those unaware that this practice is so common.

As soon as the online pharmacy scammer has all the information that he or she needs from you (or that he or she suspects you will give up), the company will suddenly disappear. You may find that the Better Business Bureau can help you, but more often than not, you can simply submit your case to the FBI for them to add to their long list of online scammers that need to be stopped. By the time your case hits the top of the list, there will be little trace left of the people who scammed you. If they are from another country, which is the case most of the time, it becomes even harder to bring these people to justice. It does not matter anyway because the scammers have already probably scammed dozens of other people just like you.

Advanced Fee Scams

These types of scams are to hard to miss if you have an e-mail account, although you may not call them by the name "advanced fee scams." What we are really talking about here is more commonly called the Nigerian scam. You may have to wonder who would ever agree to what the e-mail asks a person to do, but sadly, people around the world lose millions to the Nigerian scam every single year.

The basis of this scam, which does not have to come from Nigeria (but which usually does) is that the sender, for some reason or another, cannot get to his money. Sometimes this has to do with an inheritance. Other times it is about a large client check he wants to cash. Whatever the case, there is a business problem, and he cannot get to money that is rightfully his, and that is where you come in. The laws in America are much more lenient. Will you please cash this check and wire the money? Of course, you can take a large commission. It is his way of saying thank you for your kindness. This might be a promise of just a few thousand dollars or could be a promise of a few million.

If you agree, there will be problems with your transaction. Something will come up and you will be asked to front money for a payment they need to make. The reasoning behind this varies, but they will always ask you for money. They will usually start off with a low amount and then, later, ask you for larger amounts. They will not stop asking for money until you are out of it. Consumers get sucked in because they are always ensured that, for just a few thousand more dollars, they will get their huge reward. There is no un-cashable check or inheritance. It is just a scam, and as soon as you are out of money, they will disappear. These thieves will go to great lengths to continue assuring you that you will be paid, including sending you multiple e-mails every day and even calling you to talk about the deal over the phone.

Every once in awhile, you will actually receive a check you can cash. This is most common with smaller scams for under $100,000. However, this version of the Nigerian scam is not any less destructive. You will be asked to cash the check and then wire transfer the money (minus the fee) to the recipient. You will be asked to do this as quickly as possible to "prove you are trustworthy." In a day or two, you will find out that the check was bad. They send you forged or washed checks, which you are then responsible for repaying. In other words, the money you sent via wire transfer is lost and you, as the casher of the check, are responsible for refunding the money to your bank. By that time, the culprit will be long gone.

Although you may receive an advanced fee scam e-mail from anyone, the majority still do come from Africa, with most coming from Nigeria. Every day, the United States Secret Service receives 400 to 600 complaints via phone and mail regarding these advanced fee scams. This problem is not going to disappear any time soon.

While all this is alarming, it does not really affect your identity — or does it? Some advanced forms of this scam are now being pulled in order to steal valuable information from you, whether it is your credit card number or bank account PIN. Some use this information to falsify immigration documents, open new accounts, or drain your money, while others take an even easier route — they sell your information for a quick dollar. Thousands of people are scammed this way every year, so be wary of suspicious e-mails. You should never have to spend money to make money.

There are some common traits of advanced fee scams that you should know. Spotting these things can help determine whether or not an e-mail is a scam:

- The e-mail will probably be marked as urgent or confidential. Commonly, this is in all caps in the subject of the e-mail, as they are trying to catch your attention right off the bat.

- The e-mail will never be addressed directly to you. Anyone legitimately asking for money should know your name. Be wary about any e-mail addressed to "CEO" or "sir."

- The dollar amounts will be written out for emphasis. If an e-mail asks you to help with retrieval of THREE MILLION DOLLARS, you are most likely being scammed.

- The e-mail will come from one of the following people: someone at the Bank of Nigeria, a relative of someone deceased who has left a lot of money, a barrister or doctor, someone with a government title, a religious figure, or a member of the royal family. Of course, these people are not really who they say they are, but these are the personas most commonly used.

- The scammer will give you specific instructions on what to do next. You will need to provide lots of personal information to prove that you can be trusted with this duty. Sending this personal information is the main way your identity can be stolen in the Nigerian scam.

- In most cases, the e-mail will be sent out as a bulk e-mail to hundreds of people. Therefore, they might be filtered out into your bulk mailbox.

Do not get duped into this scam. No matter how much information they send to you, they are never going to send you the big bucks. Never. They will go to great lengths to convince you they are legitimate, including sending you papers documenting their "true" identity. These papers are all fake. Unfortunately, the Nigerian government is not cracking down on these scams as hard as they should, and many people have actually been detained in foreign countries and killed trying to chase their money. High-level government officials sometimes take part in these scams, and the result is not pretty. Stay away at all costs.

Just for fun, let us look at one of the scam "advanced fee" letters that recently came to my mailbox. I get dozens of these every day, as do most people with an e-mail address. Can you spot what makes it stand out as a scam?

SCAM EXAMPLE

Attn: Winner,

We are pleased to inform you of the release of the long awaited results of the EU-JAPAN EMAIL LOTTO [SWEEPSTAKES] PROMOTIONS lottery programmes draws held recently. You were entered unaware as an independent participants with Ticket Number: 719-226-1319 with Serial Number-902-66.Your email address attached to Lucky Draw number: 5, 12, 30, 11, 17, 43 with bonus number 25 which consequently won the ABM INTERNATIONAL LOTTERY PROMOTIONS INC organised Email lottery for and on behalf of EU-Japan Email Lotto Programmes event in the 3rd category.

You have been approved for a payment of the sum 1,500,000 (One Million, Five Hundred Thousand Euros) in cash credited to file. Reference number: EU/JP/BCC 00078653.This is from a total cash prize of 15,000,000.00 {Fifteen Million Euros} shared among the ten International winners in the 3rd categories. All participants were randomly selected through a computer ballot system drawn from 25,000 names of email users around the world, as part of their yearly international promotion program, this programme is sponsored by the conglomeration of multi-national Companies in Europe and Japan in collaboration with Computer Hardware and Software manufacturers worldwide.

Due to mix up of some names and addresses, we urge you to keep this Winning personal and discreet until your claims have been processed and your funds remitted to you, this is part of our security measures to avoid double claiming or unwarranted abuse of the system by other participants or impersonators. Your lucky Draw number fell under our European coupon booklet, thus your winning prize sum is now deposited in a special.

Account with the OFFICIAL approved European Bank based in Holland-Netherlands-Bank-POST BANK NL. To begin your claim, DO NOT contact us, instead contact the approved paying bank as they will guide you step by step until your winning prize is paid to you.

SCAM EXAMPLE

Dr. M. Richards.

Processing Department

Post Bank NL

Antwoornumer 1802, 1055AM Amsterdam-Netherlands.

Also give him the following information:

YOUR FULL NAME:

CONTACT STREET ADDRESS:

TELEPHONE NUMBERS OFFICE/MOBILE:

FAX NUMBER:

OCCUPATION:

YOUR AGE:

YOUR NATIONALITY {COUNTRY OF ORIGIN}:

Remember, your winning must be claimed as quickly as possible. Failure to claim your winning prize will obviously mean that your winning prize will be re-staked in our next lottery draws, so ensure that the needful is done now and quickly too. Once again, accept our profound and sincere congratulations on your winning.

So, what are you clues that this is fake? First and foremost, the broken and hard-to-read English should tip you off. Then, the e-mail hit all the marks noted as indications that it is fake, starting with the urgent and confidential undertones. The e-mail never addresses you personally, even though you are supposedly the big winner. They reveal the amount for emphasis and give you direct instructions as to what to do next. Spotting these scammer e-mails may not seem hard to you now that you know what you are looking for, but unfortunately, hundreds of people every day are sucked in by the promise of big money. Sometimes it is from a lottery, like this letter. Other times it is an inheritance. Still other times, it is a business deal — they just want your help in cashing a check. Whatever the case, e-mails like this are bad news. Do not reply or get pulled into their plan.

Charity Scams

In my opinion, charity scams are the worst kind. Scam artists are using your "good deeds" to make a profit and, since you are less likely to donate money twice, are effectively stealing from the legitimate charities that really do need the money. Unfortunately, charity scams are also some of the hardest to bring to justice. After all, you willingly gave up money to these people, expecting nothing in return.

Whenever there is a disaster, charity scams begin to pop up on the Internet. Sometimes, letters will arrive to your e-mail (spam). Other times, scammers will buy Internet domain names that seem to be related to the charity to fool you into believing there is an associate (spoofing). Still other times, scammers will e-mail you with a fake confirmation letter for your donation, asking you to verify your credit card number (phishing). No matter what their method, it adds up to you losing at least the amount you originally donated. That is the best-case scenario. Chances are they have stolen your credit card information as well and will make off with a lot more than your donation.

It is sad to have to look out for fake charities, but as a point in case, after Hurricane Katrina, scammers everywhere began buying domain names with the word "Katrina" in them. The same thing happened after the tsunami, and before that, the same thing happened after 9/11.

Here is what a common e-mail from a charity scammer will look like. This could be sent directly to you or posted as a message on a Web site.

Dear Concerned Citizen,

In light of the HORRIBLE tragedies that have befallen our country, we are collecting money to help the innocent victims recover their lives. Your donation can really make a difference!!!

Notice how this reads more like a sales letter than a request for donations. It is not addressed to you specifically, and the multiple exclamation points should be an indication of a scam. If you want to donate, try working with a company you know is trustworthy, like the Red Cross or a local church. If you have not heard of them, stay away.

Remember, charity scams sometimes take another form. The charity might be legitimate, but that does not mean that the person in charge is honest. Every day, people are stealing money from their employers. Unfortunately, this dishonesty is hard for us to catch. In fact, it is impossible for the average consumer to know which charity presidents, board members, and presidents are honest and which are looking for information to steal. The best we can do is attempt to prevent it and continuously check to ensure that our credit history is not showing anything strange.

A FEW OFFLINE METHODS OF IDENTITY THEFT

While this guide primarily helps you prevent identity theft online, it is important to remember that identity theft is commonly stolen in the real world as well. We may be a society in which having a computer is the norm, but thieves are not going to give up on tried-and-trued methods of identity theft that have been working for decades. In fact, online identity theft is just a very small part of the problem.

Identity theft is complex. Think of your identity as a puzzle. The completed puzzle will be a picture of you, with each tiny piece representing a sliver of information. The more pieces of the puzzle an identity thief can find, the more you are worth to him or her. The end user in an identity theft does not want to have to do a lot of work. It is going to be enough work covering his tracks when he has depleted you as a resource. So, to make more money, identity collectors try to find more and more information. While your name and driver's license number may only go for $5 or so, a file complete with your social security number, home address, health insurance information, credit history report, and more could be worth big bucks. Depending on how desirable you are (i.e., how easy of a target you will be compared to the total profit a thief can expect), your profile could sell for $500 or more. That is 100 times the price of the driver's license number. As the world is changing, people are taking extra care to protect their identities, so it is becoming harder for thieves to research you. The price of your information is ever increasing.

In order to find all this information, an identity thief will probably use both online and offline methods. That is where the following bits of information come in handy. Protecting yourself online will not do any good unless you are also savvy about the ways people can steal your identity offline. Most of these methods should not come as a surprise, yet millions of people across the United States fail to protect themselves from these dangers.

Phone Thieves

Phone thieves are really no more than phishers, but because they are talking to you instead of e-mailing you, many people more readily believe them. It is much easier to delete a suspicious e-mail than to say no to someone who has called you. Unfortunately, phone conversations are not commonly documented. You may save your e-mail to report a problem, but you probably do not record a phone conversation or even make a note of the number on your caller ID, if the number was not blocked in the first place. Phone thieves can wreak havoc without leaving a single trace behind.

A typical phone conversation may go something like what follows:

Mrs. Henry: Hello?

Caller/Scammer: Hello, may I please speak with Mrs. Henry?

Mrs. Henry: This is she.

Scammer: Hi, Mrs. Henry. This is George Perry with The Yourtown National Bank. We're having a problem with your savings account here with us.

Mrs. Henry: What's the problem? I was just in there yesterday and everything was fine!

Scammer: It appears that someone has been attempting to access your bank account online, but has failed to enter the correct password seven times in a row. We've temporarily locked down your account, as we think a hacker is trying to break into it. Do you use our online banking services, Mrs. Henry?

Mrs. Henry: No, no, I don't even have a computer. I don't even have my account set up for online banking.

Scammer: That's quite all right, Mrs. Henry. We've locked out your account so that no one can access it. What I need to do is go into your account and reactivate it, changing your personal information so that the person trying to access your account can't get in.

Mrs. Henry: Should I come into the bank?

Scammer: Actually, we can do it right over the phone to save you the trouble if you'd like. You can either bring a photo ID to the bank or verify your personal information over the phone.

Mrs. Henry: I was just there yesterday, and I don't want to drive back there again.

Scammer: That's fine. I want to quickly verify with you that I am from the bank. Your account number is 2098128970. Is this correct?

Mrs. Henry: Let me grab my checkbook...yes.

Scammer: Let's see here. I just need you to verify your birth date for me to confirm that I am, in fact, speaking with the right Mrs. Henry.

Mrs. Henry: June 2, 1959.

Scammer: Okay, great, and your social security number?

Mrs. Henry: 123-45-6789.

Scammer: Perfect. And you said that you don't have an online account set up with that checking account?

Mrs. Henry: No.

Scammer: Okay, it must be on default settings, which uses your PIN as your password and your account number as your user name. Can you confirm your PIN for me?

Mrs. Henry: 5555.

Scammer: Great. I'm on the Internet, looking at your account now and it seems that no one has broken into it. I'm going to set up a new password for you, should you ever need to get into your account. Do you have a piece of paper?

Mrs. Henry: Yes, go ahead.

Scammer: Okay, your new username is imscammed and your new password is naïve. Got that?

Of course the scammer is not going to use that as your username and password to tip you off, but can you see how easy it would be for someone to smooth talk his or her way into all sorts of personal information? Like Mrs. Henry, millions of people have been scammed this way, and the result is definitely not a good experience. Once "George" hangs up the phone, Mrs. Henry has a false sense of security. She believes there was a problem, but that someone is currently fixing it. In addition, since she just revealed that she had recently been to the bank, the scammer knows that he has even more time to play. He got her bank account number from somewhere, which is easy enough to do – it is on every check you write. By confirming with her that one bit of information, he got Mrs. Henry to tell him her birthday, social security number, and PIN number all in a few minutes. With that information, he can drain her account, and because he has the proper information, the bank will not suspect anything strange or alert Mrs. Henry. She might not know anything is wrong until she gets her next bank statement or tries to write a check that bounces.

Grab and Run

No real mystery here – some identity thieves still just grab your purse or wallet and run. Pickpockets are still common, especially in larger cities and tourist areas. Because most people carry all their personal information in their wallet, it is an easy target for thieves. You may initially be upset about losing your money, but losing your credit card, social security card, passport, and driver's license is much worse.

These kinds of thieves are smart. They do not just pick someone out of the crowd, grab your purse, and run. That is a good way to get caught, and fines are just the beginning of a thief's worries. Getting caught could also mean jail time, and most have had prior convictions or are wanted on other charges. So, they plan.

A grab-and-runner will start by looking at your purse or wallet. For a purse, they want something falling off your shoulder or held loosely in your hand. Bigger is not always better, but if it looks big without being heavy or awkward, that is a plus. Also, a thief will more likely strike someone carrying a designer purse, in which case the purse itself can also be sold. For a wallet, they look for someone who puts it in a back pocket. They will also check to see if the wallet is sticking above the pocket line, which makes reaching for it much easier. In fact, they might be able to wiggle it free without you even knowing.

You are most at risk if you are alone. If there is a big, beefy bodyguard watching your every move, the thief knows that he or she will probably get caught rather easily. Instead, if you are alone, the thief can take you by surprise and run away, leaving you with no one to help you. Having a crowd to run into is crucial, and tourists are the best targets. Tourists are usually so focused on seeing the sights that they are not paying attention to their surroundings.

People have been picking pockets since clothes first started having pockets. It is not a new trend, but unfortunately, not one that will die soon either. I have not included pickpocket tips in the long list of identity theft prevention tips in Chapter 4 simply because this is not an online issue. However, to help keep you safe, here are a few common pickpocket prevention tips to keep in mind:

- You do not have to use a fanny pack, but carry a bag that makes sense in a pickpocket-prone area. Instead of one that you wear on your back or that slings over your shoulder, look for a bag that crosses over your chest or securely sits under your arm. The bag makes all the difference.

- Never carry your social security card or passport with you when you are seeing the sites or when you are not traveling. If you must bring that sensitive information, such as may be the case if you are traveling overseas, keep it in the hotel room. Additionally, make use of the hotel safe. Maids, room service employees, and other hotel personnel may not be trustworthy, and it is hard to prove who stole your stuff if you have that problem. Lock up anything valuable, and remember – your identity is valuable.

- Do not carry cash on vacation, especially in another country. You cannot track down cash if it is stolen; plus, it is annoying to have to convert everything into the foreign currency if you are abroad. Instead, opt for traveler's checks and your credit card. Yes, your credit card will still work in many foreign countries. Before you leave on vacation, call your company to see if this is the case. If possible, you might even want to consider getting a prepaid "smart" card just for your trip. That way, thieves have less to gain from stealing the card, and you do not have to worry about overspending.

- Travel with others and stick close. Thieves are less likely to strike a group because there are more eyes watching each person in that situation.

- Use bags with zippers, not snaps, Velcro, ties, or other loose fixtures. You are more likely to feel someone from behind unzipping the bag than you are to feel someone just reaching into the bag. Keep in mind that these thieves have been stealing identities for years in some cases. They know how to move carefully so you do not notice.

- Use a smaller wallet, especially if you will not be carrying it in a purse. Men often get their wallets stolen when they stick out of the pocket a bit and can easily be seen and gently grabbed. Instead, use a wallet that is sleek and fits completely in your pocket, or do not use a wallet at all. Have your female travel companion carry your money in a secure purse.

- If you are going to carry items in a pocket, do not use a back pocket. Even side pockets on jeans or trousers do not work very well. Instead, wear cargo pants with pockets that close. You will be more likely to notice someone trying to steal something out of your pants that way.

- Do not carry all your credit cards at once. Keep a "back up" in the hotel safe so that, if your things are stolen, you have a way to survive while you sort out the mess.

Dumpster Divers

Who would have ever thought that we would live in a world where our trash should be under lock and key? That seems a bit ridiculous, right? Ridiculous, yes, but it is also true. Our garbage gives up all sorts of secrets for people who understand how to make the most of it. Dumpster divers are not just looking for fixer-upper furniture and thrown-out clothing that still has a bit of life in it. Today's dumpster divers are on the prowl for information.

Your trash is full of all sorts of sensitive information. Here are just a few of the things you can find in the average person's dumpster:

- **Credit Card Offers:** This is the big one, because most of us get dozens of credit card offers every month. They can really be dangerous if you do not shred them. While credit card offers usually do not include your social security number on them (although some might, so always check), what thieves can do is send them in with a "change of address." So, since you are pre-approved for the credit card, the thief can get some new plastic in the mail in only a matter of days. With other information that can be stolen from other sources and a bit of fast talking, anyone can take that theft to the next level. Just imagine: It all started with a credit card offer.

- **Bank Statements:** While bank statements usually don't include your social security number or your PIN, they do include your account number and balance as well as other clues in piecing together information about you.

- **Expired Driver's Licenses and ID Cards:** Although expired, some clerks never look at that and are simply interested in making sure that the face in the picture matches the name. If an identity thief looks similar to you, it can be easy for him or her to pass of the driver's license as his own. In addition, this also contains your signature and driver's license number.

- **Expired Passports:** This is as dangerous as an expired driver's license or ID card because it is a document proving your identity.

- **Credit Reports:** This is the jackpot for an identity thief. Your credit report contains just about every piece of information that someone needs to totally become you, from your social security number to your banking information. Referring to the request number on the document, the thief can also call to inquire about even more information on your credit report. Yet, thousands of people throw these in the garbage without thinking twice.

- **Luggage Tags:** These tags alone are not worth much, but paired with other information can help an identity thief put together a profile of you.

- **Old Resumes:** Using your resume, a thief can put together a work history for you, as well record your address, phone number, and e-mail address. In addition, on federal resumes, you are often required to list your social security number, which can be a goldmine for an identity thief.

- **Medical Records:** Most people don't realize just how much information someone can get from a medical record of any kind. Depending on the document, it may or may not include things like your social security number, address and phone number, doctor's name, list of prescriptions, family history, medical history, hospital stays, blood type, and so forth. This can all be used against you.

- **Travel Itineraries:** Sometimes, you create an itinerary for a trip and print and extra copy or decide that you do not need it. When you throw it away, however, you are not only telling thieves when you will not be at home (and thus when you will be most susceptible to identity theft), but you are also telling them where you will be at all times. By calling a hotel and pretending to be you, a thief can learn all sorts of information. It just takes a little creativity.

- **Old Tax Information:** Again, by using old tax

documents, or even copies of them, an identity thief can learn lot of information about you. By fitting these pieces of the puzzle together, your identity will be worth a lot more money to any end user who wishes to purchase an identity.

- **Utility Bills:** By grabbing old copies of your utility bills, an identity thief can infiltrate your account, set up new accounts, and add pieces of information to your complete identity package.

Any document that contains account numbers, your name and address, your signature, personal information about your whereabouts, medical information, employment history, or social security number needs to be shredded. Thieves are versatile – they will work with what you give them. Invest in a shredder and use it whenever needed. After all, it only takes a few seconds to shred a document, but it can take years to recover from identity theft.

Skimming

Identity theft is not always as easy to detect as you might think. Skimming is something that is done through what would otherwise be legitimate reasons. These kinds of occurrences happen when a person has access to credit cards of others. This might happen with employees who are not trustworthy and who might steal from others.

There are several ways it works. The basics of the scam are simple. A person must gain access to your credit card through legitimate means, and then copy down the numbers or otherwise keep track of the credit card numbers to use later. In order to have the credit card number, a person must have the credit card. This happens in stores, hotels, and restaurants. Most of the time, it is found in situations where an employee has access to a credit card when the customer is not looking. This might very well be at a restaurant, after someone has given the credit card to the person to pay for their meal. When they can take the card away from the customer, this could be the chance to write down the numbers. In order to use a credit card later on, a person will have to have the numbers off the front of the card, as well as the numbers that are found on the back of the card. They will take these numbers and then return the card to the owner. The person will not know that their number have been stolen – and will not find out until the thief uses their card.

There are other ways that skimming can be pulled off. Sometimes, a thief might use photographs of credit cards as others use them. This is something that has been done a couple of times. An employee will take a photograph of the credit card so that they can get the numbers off of it later on.

There are also devices that can be used to steal these numbers. Sometimes, skimming is done when an electronic device is attached to a card reader itself. This device is not put onto the card reader by the people who own the card reader. It is attached by a thief, who then has the access to all of the numbers that they got off of the card reader. This is something that can cause a lot of damage because a person can put their device on something like an ATM, and get hundreds of numbers that they can use later on.

Skimming is something that is difficult to protect yourself from, because you aren't doing anything that could be considered dangerous with your credit card. You are using it just as you should be using it. However, you still have to worry about skimming taking place in just about any situation.

The best way to protect yourself against skimming is to be vigilant with your credit card statements and with your bank statements. Be sure that you are checking them regularly, and that you are reporting problems to your bank.

A FEW SCENARIOS: HOW ONE SLIP-UP COULD BE WORTH THOUSANDS

No one is trying to scare you, but one tiny mistake can cost you thousands of dollars and ruin your credit. It does not help matters to be paranoid that every person you meet is going to try to steal your identity. At the same time, that is absolutely something to worry about – while most people will not try to steal your identity, almost everyone in your life has the chance to do so. Feeling overwhelmed? That is not a bad thing. Preventing identity theft is only effective if you go at it full force, and to feel passionate about identity theft prevention, you have to feel a little scared about the possibilities. Read through the following scenarios. These are not far-fetched ideas – they show you how just one mistake can make for your ultimate demise. While the names and exact events of the following scenarios are fictional, versions of these situations have happened to millions of people across the country. These scenarios are why identity theft prevention education is important for everyone.

Scenario #1: From Junk Mail to Jail

Mary worked the night shift at the local gas station, so before she headed into work she left a note for her husband to put out the trash before he went to bed. She got home to find that the neighbor's loose dog had ripped the bag apart. Garbage was scattered all over her lawn, and Mary, tired from a night of work, slowly picked up the litter. This was only the beginning of her bad luck, however.

When Mary's trash was scattered across the lawn, an opportunist (we will call him Mark) walking by peeked into the bag and saw some pieces of junk mail that had not been shredded. Stuffing the envelope into his pocket was easy, and because it was so late at night, he did not draw any attention to himself. Once home, Mark opened Mary's mail to see how he could make use of the pre-screened credit card offers.

Within a week, the thief had applied for four different cards, making sure to change his address on each of them.

That is when the real fun began. With each of the cards, he set up online accounts to track his spending in Mary's name. Mark then decided to dig a bit deeper. Using Mary's home address, he sent her a letter printed on the credit card's company letterhead, easy enough to create from online images. The letter stated that he was an employee of the credit card company and he believed that someone had opened a fraudulent account in Mary's name. Could she please use the enclosed number or e-mail address to contact him right away?

When Mary e-mailed him the next day, Mark "verified" that she had an account with the company by giving her the login information for the very account he had set up. He then asked Mary to confirm her social security number to see if it was the one that matched the account, which she could clearly see was working and using her information. Mary, hoping to clear up the information right away, gladly e-mailed Mark her social security number. He confirmed the fraudulent account and said that it would be cleared up in a few days. He said that she may want to wait a few months before checking her credit history report because it would still show the weird charges, but that he would be in close contact with her and the authorities during this time.

Mary took that advice and, since she was not checking her credit score, Mark had a field day with her social security number. He had his girlfriend use it to apply for a car loan, took out a personal loan at the bank, and opened six more credit cards in Mary's name. After about two months, he cashed in all that he could with the credit cards using their "fast cash" options, sold the car to an unknowing private buyer, and skipped town. Before he was done, he also sold her social security number to an immigrant in the area whose visa was soon going to expire so that she could use it to get a job. By the time Mary figured out something was wrong, the police were knocking on her door, as she had not paid bills, returned phone calls, or responded to lenders in over three months.

She was also wanted on drug charges. Mark's girlfriend, using Mary's identity, was caught selling cocaine to an undercover police officer. Mark used money from the fraudulent loans and credit cards to bail her out of jail and, when the couple drove away, the police had no way to find them again. Mary was a criminal, but not really. It will take Mary a lifetime to fix the problems caused by Mark and his girlfriend, and it all started with one piece of junk mail.

Scenario #2: The Perfect Date

Frustrated with trying to meet men at bars, Susan decided to give online dating a try. She signed up for both free and paid services on some of the most popular dating services and, after a few weeks, had formed casual friendships with a number of other users looking for love on the Internet. One guy stood out to her more than all the others. His name was Jeff, and after just one e-mail, Susan knew that Jeff was someone she wanted to get to know.

Over the course of about a month, Jeff and Susan's

friendship blossomed to the point where Jeff was talking to Susan every single day on instant messenger, via e-mail, and even with phone calls. Susan was from New York and Jeff from Kansas, but he told her that he had grown up in New York City, so they quickly found things to talk about. Jeff was coming out of a bad relationship with a girl who took him for granted, and, like Susan, he was tired of going to bars to try to find a nice girl. Susan had known Jeff for about six weeks when he started to send her gifts at work and home. They were small trinkets, as Jeff did not have a lot of money, but it made Susan feel special when Jeff sent her flowers in front of her co-workers.

They never seemed to run out of things to say, and by the time their friendship hit the two-month mark, Jeff admitted he was falling in love with Susan. Both agreed that the next step was a face-to-face meeting to talk about possible relocation, but there were two problems. Jeff did not have the money for a plane ticket and Susan did not have vacation time at work so she could not travel. Jeff suggested that Susan pay for his ticket to travel to her and he would pay her back for half when he could. After all, they were going to be spending a lifetime together, probably. Jeff hinted that he was ready to settle down and have children in the near future.

So, Susan logged online, beaming from ear to ear, and loaded her credit card information into the airport's system. She then e-mailed Jeff her username and password so that he could buy the airplane ticket. She logged on to make sure things had gone well and, sure enough, Jeff had purchased one round-trip ticket as they had agreed. The couple continued to chat online, and Susan felt more and more anticipation as the day of Jeff's travels to her neared.

Susan waited at the airport for Jeff's flight, nervous and happy at the same time. They announced that the flight had landed and she waited by the gate, looking for a face that was similar to the pictures Jeff had sent. Susan did not see anyone that fit the description. Confused, she wandered to luggage claim – perhaps he had slipped past her and was waiting there. No one seemed to be looking for her. Jeff's cell phone was turned on and rang when she called, but he did not pick up the phone. So, Susan went to the service desk. Perhaps he had missed his flight.

What the customer service rep told Susan made her gasp in horror. Not only had Jeff not made the flight, but he had also changed the ticket the night before to be heading to Mexico the next day. In addition, using Susan's account, there had been another ticket purchased to Mexico, and it had landed about an hour ago, meaning that Jeff and his traveling friend were probably already long gone. A call to the Mexican airport confirmed just that. There was no way for the police to know where they had gone.

Susan immediately called her credit card company to see if there was anything they could do, and she found that Jeff had also used her card and information, found in the airport Web site's profile, to make thousands of dollars worth of other online purchases. She would not be held accountable for those purchases, but she would not be refunded for the airline expenses, because she had authorized his use of that account by giving him the credit card. Susan never heard from Jeff again, but she spent the next year working overtime to pay off the fees for the two plane tickets and the hundreds of dollars in fees that she was charged for changing the tickets at the last minute, as well as the interest on her credit card for not being able to pay off the full balance right away. Jeff – if that really was his name – stole over $3,000 from her and will probably never be caught.

Scenario #3: Connecting the Dots

Craig, an avid Internet user, was an active member at a number of online forums, Web sites, and so forth. One day, he decided to subscribe to an online newsletter for a hockey Web site. The site required him to register using his e-mail address, a password of his choice, and some personal information like his address, sex, and phone number. So, our hockey-lover signed up, not even thinking twice about why an online hockey newsletter would need that information.

In fact, because the registration form had him use his e-mail address as his username, Craig just naturally used the same password that he used for his e-mail. What Craig did not know is that this was exactly what the Web site's owner, Heather, was hoping would happen. When Craig hit "submit" on the registration online, he was not signing up for a hockey newsletter. He was sending his e-mail address and password to Heather. Although not everyone signing up at this site used the same password as they used for their e-mail, many did as an automatic response to the e-mail username. Of those who did not, many used a similar version. If their e-mail password was hello123, for example, their password on the site might be 123hello.

From that, it was not hard for Heather to take information sent from Craig and other users to log into their e-mail accounts. Once there, it was not hard to figure out where Craig had online accounts. She saw that he used PayPal for eBay purchases, did online banking, and even paid his credit card online. Although Craig did not save his e-mails with passwords to any of these sites, Heather did not have to break a sweat figuring them out.

Go to any site and pretend you do not know the password. These login sites all have built-in password protection, but they also have ways to find a lost password. Usually, one of the most basic ways to retrieve your password is to have it e-mailed to you. All Heather had to do was submit that help ticket, sign in to Craig's e-mail, and retrieve the password. Even the "secret questions" did not help protect Craig. For someone who wants to steal your identity, doing a bit of research to find your mother's maiden name, your paternal grandmother's name, the town you were born in, or your elementary school is worth that extra time. So, really, it is not very hard. Online resources list this information about just about everyone. All you need is an address to confirm that the information is really about the person in question. Heather had everything she needed from Craig's registration form.

She did not get very far because Craig caught the weird online transactions fairly quickly. However, in just a few days, Heather had spent over $1,000 on eBay purchases and even more using his credit card number. Unfortunately, Craig did not even have a name to give the police. Even if he could have tracked the culprit to the online hockey newsletter, he had no idea that a girl named Heather was behind the scam. Furthermore, the site was wiped clean and parked at a generic advertising site. Heather had also registered it privately. In 48 hours, she got away with money and ruining Craig's credit, all because he wanted the latest in hockey news sent straight to his inbox.

Scenario #4: A Good Cause

Jan was the type of girl who would do anything for just about anyone. She worked a 40-hour workweek to provide for her sick mother and then spent nights at the soup kitchen. She went to church every Sunday and always remembered to send her siblings and college friends' birthday cards. Jan was just one of those ladies who you wanted to know, and she wanted to know you, too.

Jan was horrified to learn about the widespread destruction in the south due to Hurricane Katrina, so she saved up for weeks to be able to give her donation. She planned to give her $1,000 donation straight to the Red Cross, but she received an e-mail from an organization called Help Katrina that asked if she would consider donating. She checked out their Web sites, which had a lot of great Katrina-related facts, and they allowed her to use PayPal to submit a donation, which was very convenient for Jan, since she often sold items on eBay and had a balance in her PayPal account that she wanted to spend. Help Katrina was the perfect option.

So, Jan clicked on the PayPal button on the organization's Web site, logged in, and designated $1,000 to the charity. She received a confirmation e-mail, which she printed for her tax records, and, feeling good about giving to a worthy cause, went to bed. All seemed well until the following week, when she got a call from a Help Katrina official. Identifying herself as Pamela, the caller referenced Jan's donation and said that there had been a small problem – the donation had not gone through correctly. She told Jan that, if she would log onto her PayPal account, she should see that the money had bounced back to her PayPal account. While on the phone with Pamela, Jan did just that – and sure enough, the $1,000 was credited to her account. The payment had not gone through for some reason.

Would she like to donate via credit or debit card? Pamela assured her that a card payment would go through immediately. Jan agreed. She could simply withdraw the money from PayPal to pay off her credit card at the end of the month. It did not really matter to her how the money got to the charity. It just mattered that the money made its way to the people who really needed it. So, she gave Pamela her credit card information and asked that they send her a receipt. Pamela assured Jan that it was in the mail.

What Jan did not realize is that her original PayPal payment had not "bounced back" to her account. She had never paid it in the first place. The PayPal button on the "charity" Web site was nothing more than a redirect to a Web site page that simply looked like the PayPal login page, but it was not. The PayPal information was spoofed and Jan had given her login information to Pamela (whose real name was most likely something else). In addition, she had also given her full credit card information to this Pamela over the phone. It was only a matter of time before everything went up in flames.

Pamela and her fake Help Katrina site began by using Jan's credit card for the $1,000 donation. That money, which should have been going to disaster relief, went into Pamela's "big screen TV" fund. At this point, Jan did not suspect anything was wrong. After all, she had given Help Katrina the authority to take $1,000 from her credit card account. The indication that something was wrong did not happen until three days later. Suddenly, all at once, Jan's entire PayPal account was drained and her credit card was maxed out buying big-ticket items online with rush delivery. Before Jan could stop them, the items were delivered to the PO Box and Pamela was gone.

Jan had to put her charity work on hold while she worked to pay off the fraudulent charges – with her card, they were not all covered by the consumer protection plan, especially since they were made online. Her total losses, not counting the lost $1,000 that did not go to her charity, were around $10,000 when the interest was added to that mix. It took Jan years to pay it off and even longer to rebuild her credit. Jan thought she was doing something good for the world, but because she was not a savvy Internet user, she was sucked into a horrible situation.

Scenario #5: Winning the Lottery

Joe never considered himself a lucky person. In fact, he always seemed to lose money when gambling, and after 40 years of playing the lottery, he never won more than a few dollars here and there. It did not really matter. Joe was a successful mortgage broker and he believed in making your own luck.

Until, that is, Joe got an e-mail one day telling him that he had won a Nigerian lottery and was eligible for over ten million dollars (TEN MILLION DOLLARS) in prize money. He was skeptical. Joe had heard about advanced fee scams and he did not want to be pulled into one because he knew that they did not end well for the so-called benefactor of the money. However, against his better judgment, Joe decided to respond to the e-mail. Replying would do no harm, right? He was not going to give them any money. Joe just wanted to see what this e-mail was all about.

He received an answer to his reply right away. Yes, Joe had won the lottery in Nigeria, and no, this was not one of those weird online scams. Joe was actually, unbeknownst to him, entered into the Nigerian lottery every week and his name just happened to get pulled this week for the big prize. There were no costs and nothing to worry about. Joe just had to confirm his identity and the prize money would be all his.

I am sure by now that you know Joe is going to get scammed. He replied to the e-mail, wanting to know more about the lottery, and all his questions were answered promptly. After he was urged to submit his information as soon as possible for fear of forfeiting the prize, Joe e-mailed the lottery organizers with his bank account information. The entire balance would be wired as soon as possible.

Before the week was up, Joe got another e-mail. Something was wrong with his lottery winnings. Another person with the same name and birthday had also come forward to claim the prize. Would Joe be willing to confirm his identity further by transferring a very minimal amount of money to the lottery's bank account? If by chance there was a mix-up, they would wire that full amount back immediately, but they suspected that the other person was a scam artist out to steal Joe's money, so they were sure that he would not even agree to the transfer. Not wanting to seem like a phony, Joe agreed and sent over the "small" fee of $5,000. Of course, that amount did not seem small to Joe at the time, but he was willing to make that sacrifice for now since he was going to be receiving over ten million dollars in a week or two.

Problem after problem arose with the transaction, and Joe continued to send relatively small amounts of money to help the proceedings along. Finally, the lottery representative asked Joe for a favor. They had been working closely for almost four months at this point, and Joe had even spoken to him on the phone on multiple occasions. The Nigerian government was holding the money for some reason. If they sent Joe the full amount for all their lotteries – over 100 million – could he take out what was owed to him, the ten million, and wire the rest to the next winner? It would make the process finished completely once and for all.

Luckily for Joe, he had the good sense (finally) to talk to his bank. As soon as he started explaining the proceedings, his banker stopped Joe and explained to him that he needed to call the FBI right away. He was being scammed. If the company did send a check, it was bound to be a fake one, and Joe could be held liable for any amount he cashed. Joe got out before he was in millions of dollars over his head, but he did lose about $12,000 in the process. That is not a small chunk of change.

Something even more horrifying came to light as Joe began to really look at the situation with a clear head. On many of their proceedings, Joe had used his social security number, birthday, and driver's license number to take care of issues with the transactions. A quick call to the credit reporting bureaus confirmed it – these scammers were making good use of Joe's identity. Over the next 20 years, Joe continued to find ways in which these scammers were ruining his life. His social security number and other personal information were sold and he could not get back the thousands he spent to try to retrieve his millions in lottery winnings. You might have already guessed it, but when Joe questioned them about it, poof. They were gone. Suddenly, the phone numbers, e-mail addresses, and names of the people he had known for four months now seemed to have never existed in the first place.

And that is how most identity thieves are. One hint that they might get caught and they will disappear forever with your money and your identity.

STRAIGHT FROM THE EXPERT'S MOUTH: IDTHEFTSECURITY.COM TALKS ABOUT PREVENTION

In 1992, when Robert Siciliano started selling information videos, audio tapes, and non-lethal personal protection products, he could not have imagined how personal and business identity theft would evolve over the years, especially through use of the Internet. Today, Siciliano is the CEO of **IDTheftSecurity.com**, one of the world's leaders in personal identity theft protection. **IDTheftSecurity. com** provides citizens, corporations and associations privacy and personal security information and practical solutions to prevent crime. With Siciliano at the helm, their business model has changed from one providing protection products to a full-blown informational company that provides personal security seminars and training across the country.

Says Siciliano, "We've witnessed greater media coverage and a major rise in fraud, scams and theft as information continues to become more available." And that is a good thing. As the public becomes more and more aware of security threats and the tactics used by identity thieves, we can, as a culture, better learn to stop them in their tracks. Although Siciliano has seen lots of identity theft trends over the past decade, there is one he has not seen – a decline in popularity in any category. That means that there are more identity thieves out there, and that they are becoming smarter.

What is the most popular form of identity theft? There are no surprises here. "Phishing for dollars. Identity thieves send out millions of e-mails daily requesting victim's usernames, passwords, cash and credit cards and countless ways," says Siciliano.

However, the biggest mistake that people make regarding identity may surprise you, as it is not related to phishing. Says Siciliano, "Most people put up enough information about themselves on various social network sites that a thief can use it against them." Web sites like MySpace and Facebook have given identity thieves a whole new way to attack their victims. Experts are seeing trends in this, but the public seems to be creating new and more detailed public profiles every day.

Another major problem with identity security that Siciliano and **IDTheftSecurity.com** are trying to combat is the unprotected status of many online shopping Web sites. Although there are thousands – probably millions – of online sites that are secure, Siciliano warns that there is no way to be completely sure. The key, as they teach at their **IDTheftSecurity.com** seminars and training sessions, is being proactive and suspecting identity theft before it happens. Customers are responsible for checking their credit card statements and reporting anything strange.

Like other security expert, Siciliano agrees that there are changes that need to be made in identity securities policies and laws. However, there are things that the average consumer can do to prevent theft on a high level. His number one identity theft prevention tip?

"Make sure your PC's security definitions are updated and make sure there aren't P2P programs installed on your PCs that can allow all your computers data to be shared with the world."

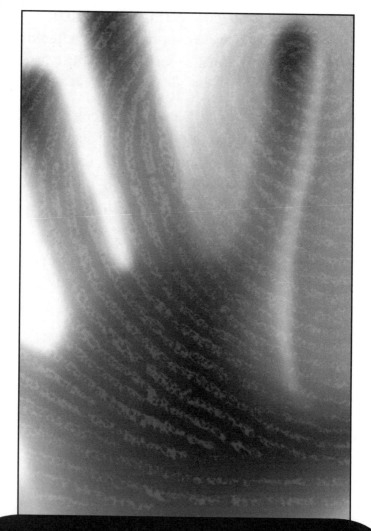

Remember to always protect your social security number. This is a valuable piece of information. If the wrong person discovers it, then it could cost you thousands of dollars.

4

PREVENTION — 99 TIPS FOR PROTECTION FROM IDENTITY THIEVES

Imagine that your identity is stolen. Let us assume that the criminal was smart and really took you for all you are worth. You lose thousands of dollars out of your savings account. Ten credit cards were opened in your name, with purchases totaling over $50,000. Your credit score may well have been flushed down the drain. In fact, the FBI has a warrant out for your arrest and armed officers show up on your doorstep to arrest you. How could this have happened?

You may never know. Somehow, your social security number and other crucial information, like your address and birth date, became common knowledge. The really upsetting issue here is that, no matter how your identity was stolen, by taking a few extra precautions it could have been avoided. In most cases, criminals are not that smart. Victims are just naïve about their identity and how to protect it.

The fact that you are even reading this guide is a good sign. It means that you are ready to be on the offense about your identity, which is the smartest thing you can do. As a victim, your options are really limited. It can take years — decades even — to clear your name after your identity is stolen. Even then, you may find it impossible to obtain certain clearances. An identity theft is a black spot on your name for life.

The following is a comprehensive list of tips for protecting your identity online —prevention before it is even stolen in the first place. Keep in mind that the face of the Internet is changing every day. Criminals are coming up with new ways to steal your identity. So, although this is a list of the very best prevention tips, you should always keep up with consumer credit news. That is tip number one:

1. Stay up-to-date with all the new ways people are trying to scam you —and learn what you can do to stop them.

The following tips are separated into categories to help you remember them. However, do not make the mistake of thinking that certain categories do not apply to you, because they do. Use all these tips to protect your private information.

PASSWORDS AND PINS

2.   If you have the option to use a PIN or password, take it. Check with your different accounts — some allow you to set an extra password or use another PIN for an extra level of security.

3.   Choose a password that you do not have to write down. Some people like to keep a file hidden on their computer, listing passwords for various sites. This is super dangerous. No matter how well you think you have that file hidden, a hacker can find it. Writing it down on a piece of paper somewhere is just as dangerous. Make sure that the only place you have the passwords to your accounts is in your memory. After all, if you forget them, you can always go through an identification procedure to recover your password. That process is much easier than dealing with identity theft.

4.   Do not use a password that can be easily associated with you. Yes, it is hard to remember a random password, but your address, your middle name, your birthday, and your phone number are the first things people will guess. Pick something totally random. Here are some ideas for good passwords and some examples of bad passwords — keep in mind that each should also include special characters and numbers:

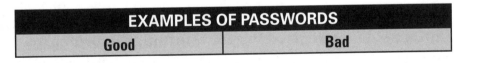

EXAMPLES OF PASSWORDS	
Good	Bad

EXAMPLES OF PASSWORDS	
Your pet's name	Your screen name
Your favorite movie	Your mother's maiden name
Your favorite number	The last four digits of your phone number
A town where you grew up	Your social security number
An activity you enjoy	Your spouse's name
The time you were born	Your birthday
Your boss's last name	Your own last name
Your favorite color or song	Anything generic (like "admin" or "test")
A day of the week	Your address

The more random the better when it comes to passwords. Choose something you can remember, but focus on security as well.

5.   Choose a different PIN or password for everything. Again, this is more difficult to remember, but it will be harder for identity thieves to crack into your life if you use lots of different passwords.

6.   Resist the urge to use a variation of the same password as well. For example, if your PIN is 4297, do not make your e-mail password "44229977" and an online account password "amy4297." Once an identity theft cracks the first password, this is the password he or she will try for every account you have. When that does not work, he or she will try variations next.

7.   Remember, when you sign up for an account online, such as registering for a forum, the owner may be able to see your password, so it is especially crucial to use something different in these cases. Try to think of your information in terms of "sensitive" and "non-sensitive." Yes, it would be annoying if someone logged into a message board to post under your name — but it is not as big of a threat to you when compared to someone figuring out the password for your online banking account. Here is a list of what is sensitive and what is not:

EXAMPLES OF PASSWORDS	
Sensitive	**Not Sensitive**
E-mail accounts	Hobby message boards
Gaming sites connected to an account	All other gaming sites
Paypal or online banking accounts	"Play" banking (stock market games)
eBay profiles	MySpace profiles
Blogs where you are the admin	All other blogs

8.   Use a password with at least eight characters. If you can use more, do so. However, avoid using a single, long word. Think about it — say you use the password "excalibur." If a thief figures out "e-x-c-a-l" and knows that your password is nine letters long, it will be fairly easy to guess the rest. Here are some examples of good ways to use long words:

• With a number or special character in the middle of the word (excal23ibur)

• With half of the word, but not the whole word, backwards (excalrubi)

- Spelled incorrectly (excallyber)

- With numbers or special characters replacing letters (exca!ibur)

- With all the vowels moved to the end of the word (xclbreaiu)

- Flip-flopped (iberexcal)

- Moving your fingers one key to the right or left (rcvs;onit)

9.   To go along with the above hint, no matter how many characters you use, mix it up. Choose both numbers and letters and, if possible, special characters (such as * or !).

10.   Use both upper and lowercase letters if the account allows it. The more variety you use with your password, the better. Think about using uppercase letters in unusual ways. Instead of in the beginning of a word (Excalibur) or every other letter (ExCaLiBuR), which people commonly do, try something like exCaliBur.

11.   Chose your secret questions and answers wisely. Most sites will give you a choice. Do not choose your mother's maiden name or your spouse's middle name. This is information that is readily available for those who really want to find it. Even your pet's name is at risk if a thief accesses records at a vet's office. Chose an answer that very few people other than yourself would be able to answer, such as your favorite teacher's name. If you can make up your own question, make it even harder. A good question, for example, would be "What is the mascot of your favorite team of your favorite sport?" Stuck on thinking of a question? Here are some great ones you can use:

- Who was my best friend in third grade?

- What was my least favorite subject in school?

- Who was my first boss?

- What is my favorite band's first album called?

- Where did I go for vacation in 2005?

- What food do I like to get at my favorite restaurant?

- What is my favorite alcoholic drink?

- Where was my best friend born?

- How many friends came to my last birthday party?

- What was my son for Halloween last year?

- Who is my favorite movie star?

- What was my grandmother's favorite thing to bake?

- Who was my role model as a child?

- What 80s fashion do I wish we could bring back?

Have fun with it! Try to think of a question to which you will know the answer right away, but which will stump anyone who does not know you well. Beware of secret questions that have a limited number of answers. For example, if you use "Who is my son's favorite Ninja Turtle?" anyone trying to steal your identity will not have to know the answer — they will just have to guess four times.

12. Do not save your passwords — clear your cookies (cache) every time you shut down your computer. This is especially crucial if you have a laptop that you use outside your home. It is fairly easy to steal something so small and compact like a laptop bag.

13. Change your passwords every six months. Some accounts will prompt you to do this, but many will not. Take matters into your own hands and simply spend one minute making a new password. In fact, you may want to note it on your day planner or calendar. Get on a schedule for changing all your passwords to keep them protected.

14. Limit those who have access to your password.
In fact, unless you share an account with a spouse, do not share that information with anyone. Some of the most tragic cases of identity theft are those in which the victims know the person stealing the identity. Children, spouses, other relatives, and close friends may all be desperate enough to steal your personal information. Do not let your guard down, even around people you think you can trust.

15. If you verbally use your PIN or password, such as you may need to do to verify your account over the phone, change it immediately afterwards. There may have been people who overheard your conversation, and you must also be aware that the operator who verified your info now has it. In addition, telephones are not completely secure. It is still possible to pick up reception from other conversations. It does not happen often on its own, but if you know what you are doing with electronics, you can figure out how to intercept and pick up other conversations.

16. Set up a special e-mail account that you can use purely for confirming registrations for non-sensitive sites like chat rooms and online celebrity fan sites. The more you can keep these Web sites separate from the ones that really matter, like your online bank account, the better.

17. An Extra–Long Tip: Make Your Password Something That You Can Remember!

Why do so any people use passwords like "Name123" that

are extremely easy for identity thieves to crack? One reason – they are easy to remember. Many people are worried that they will forget important passwords, especially if they change them all of the time. It's true – passwords can be difficult to remember. That is why most sites have "backdoor" methods for getting into your account – by answering a question, you can gain access to your account. However, this is not always the case, and, even if it is the case, forgetting your password every time you log into a site can really waste a lot of time. Therefore, it is important to create a password that you can actually remember. Following are some tips for creating great passwords...but ones that you can remember.

18. Have a theme to all of your passwords that makes sense to you but would be hard for anyone else to guess. For example, your "theme" might be "girls on my high school field hockey team." As much as they searched, few thieves would come up with that list of names. However, if that is easy for your to remember, use the names and numbers of all of the girls you played field hockey with as your passwords for a site. So, when you change from Debbie29Myerson to CandiceCandySmithstone26, you will have a little kick start to remember how you changed it. Give each password site a theme like this – just do not use something that is common to everyone. For example, "places I've been and the years I traveled there" is a good theme. "fruits and their colors" is not. Paris1985Texas is a much better password than yellowbananas.

19. Save your passwords in a master document. Yes,

this sounds like a bad tip, but it can be a good one – if you password protect this document, as well as hide it on your computer. Do not use the word "password" or "username" anyways in the document, including in the name, which will make it hard for anyone to search for it. Reserve a very, very high level password to protect it. Change this password weekly, if not more often. Yes, you will have to remember this one password – but remembering one is easier than remembering 20 or 30.

20. Create passwords for each site based on a song or poem, using lines. For example, say you used the song "Jingle Bells." The first line of that song is "Jingle Bells, Jingle Bells, Jingle all the way," which has eight letters and 39 characters. Your first password for a site could be "jbjb8jatw29". The second line of the song is "Oh what fun it is to ride" (seven words and 19 characters), so when you change your password, you can make it "owf7iitr19". Use a different song for each site where you need a password. It is a great way to create very hard passwords that are easy to remember.

21. Think of a number you can remember and a password that you can remember that has ten letters. Let us say, for example, that you use your phone number (seven digits) and the word "bookkeeper". Each letter in the word is numbered (1-b, 2-o, 3-o, 4-k, and so forth) and then you use your secret number to rearrange the letters. So, if your phone number is 555-2984, your password would be kkkoepk. Add in a number you can remember to make it a bit stronger and you have an excellent password.

PROTECTION FROM HACKING AND SPYWARE

22.   Make sure you have an anti-virus program on your computer, as well as anti-spyware protection. Symantec is a really good option, or you can ask a professional for help in choosing the best program.

23.   When available, download updates from your anti-virus company. Computer hackers are evolving every day, so protection programs have to constantly update to stay a step ahead. You should get automatic notifications to your e-mail or on your desktop when new updates are available. Download immediately.

24.   Do not download anything from the Internet unless you know exactly what it is. Many times, spyware is disguised as anti-spyware programs meant to protect you.

25.   If you meet someone online, do not download anything from them, including a picture they want to show you or a song they want you to hear. Instead, ask that they upload the picture to a free online photo site and send you the link or find the song on YouTube and allow you to listen to it that way.

26.   Stay away from P2P (Peer to Peer) online file sharing Web sites. This can be very dangerous, as you can never be sure what you are downloading along with the file. In addition, many files shared in the Peer to Peer world are not legally allowed to be share. You can receive fines of thousands and thousands of dollars for downloading things that are copyrighted, like songs.

27.   If you want to use a credit card online, make sure the site is secure first. Otherwise, the message could be caught and used. When is a site secure? When it is encrypted. Encryption should be used whenever you send an e-mail as well. Basically, what encryption does is scramble your message (an e-mail, a credit card number, etc.) so that, if it is intercepted, it cannot be read. Only the intended receiver can read the message. All you have to do to ensure that a Web site is encrypting your information is look in the lower right-hand corner of the Web browser's screen. If you see a little lock, you are safe.

28.   Ask questions. If you are unsure about a site's encryption methods or want more information, call the company before using your credit card online. If they will not answer your questions, you can always buy the item somewhere else or mail a check instead. Here are some great questions to ask if you cannot find the answers online:

• Has your site had any problems in the past?

• Will I be e-mailed the transaction details?

• What encryption methods do you use?

- Who can see my account details?

- How long has your site been in operation?

- How will you be alerted if there is a problem?

- How will I be alerted if there is a problem?

- Who is responsible for charges if there is a security problem on your site?

- How long do you keep my information?

- If I request a refund, will it be charged to my card?

If the Web site is at all ambiguous, save your shopping for another day.

29.   Consider purchasing a program than encrypts the files on your computer as well. The Web company Pretty Good Privacy (**www.pgp.com**) sells fairly inexpensive software that allows you to "lock" your computer. It is a good idea if you will be traveling, using a laptop at college, or otherwise are afraid that your computer could be stolen.

30.   Use a firewall to alert you before your computer automatically downloads anything or to prevent suspicious downloads altogether. Most anti-virus or anti-spyware programs have a firewall system, but you may have to manually set up that part of the program. Otherwise, the settings may not be optimized for you and your needs.

31.   If you choose to connect to a wireless network, make sure that network is secure. You should need a password or PIN to log onto that network. If you are going to set up your own wireless network, make it a secure one.

32.   Use a single credit card for buying things online. Keep the credit limit on this card low and patrol it often to make sure you do not see any weird activity. Avoid using a card with a high limit, using a debit card, or using multiple cards for online activity.

AVOIDING ONLINE SCAMS

33.   Only do business at auction sites that have a good reputation, like eBay. These sites offer the most support when something goes wrong and have taken measures to prevent scammers from succeeding. At the very least, you can be assured that the site itself will not scam you. If you are unsure about a site, here are some questions you may want to ask. Use the site's e-mail system, call the provided phone number (there should be one), or scan the FAQs (Frequently Asked Questions) for answers:

- How long has this site been running?

- Who is in charge (get a name, address, and phone number)?

- How many members are participating as buyers or sellers?

- Have there been any online scams on this site in the past?

- What encryption methods do you use?

- When I sign up, who gets to see my password and credit card information?

- Will I be e-mailed if there is any account activity?

- What kind of rating system is used for sellers?

- Do you have a site-wide escrow service available? If so, who runs that service and how long has it been in operation?

- What happens if there is a security problem?

- Who do I notify if my item is not what I ordered?

- What do you do if my item is not what I ordered?

- How do I report a problem?

34. Use an escrow service with large purchases. Sending money orders is a way to prove you made the payment, but it does not guarantee you will get an item. An escrow service will hold your money and/or the item and then distribute the money and item to both parties. Using a third party like that prevents anyone from not paying or from taking the money without sending the items.

35. Make sure that the escrow service you use is a reputable one. Be very, very, very wary of using an escrow service you have never heard about. It could simply be a makeshift Web site intent on collecting your credit card number. In most cases, large Web sites that run auctions and other bidding services where members trade items provide an online escrow service. While there is usually a fee for using this service, if it is run by the auction site itself, you can at least know that it is reputable. Suggest using this service and, if the other person refuses, be a bit wary of doing business with that person.

36. Check out user ratings before you buy anything from an online auction. This is not a guarantee, but it is a good way to at least spot suspicious activity. Be careful of any seller who has a low rating or is suddenly selling a very expensive item after hundreds of very small items.

37. If you receive an e-mail asking for any kind of personal information, do not reply or follow any links to Web sites. Instead, call your financial institution to make sure the e-mail is real. Financial companies will rarely e-mail you to ask for information.

38.   Never reply to any e-mails saying that your account has been suspended or frozen. Again, call the financial institution to respond to such e-mails.

39.   When you call a company to confirm an e-mail, make sure you use a phone number that has been confirmed as correct. Better yet, stop in at a brick-and-mortar office building if possible. Do not use any phone numbers or e-mail addresses that have been included in the e-mail you have received. 99 percent of the time, these will just lead right back to the scammer who will confirm that they are legitimate and ask for your personal information once again.

40.   Use a bulk mailbox folder. Keep your settings as aggressive as possible and simply check it every day to look for legitimate e-mails that appeared there by mistake. It is much easier to think of your bulk mailbox as a "holding ground" for "possible spam." If you keep on track by checking it every day, you should not have a problem with build-up. After a few days, you will be able to scan rather quickly. Non-spam e-mails will stick out like a sore thumb.

41.   If any spam e-mail ends up in your inbox, mark it as spam so your computer can learn which IP addresses are spam. Computer programs are "smart," which means that they do learn if you allow them to do so. By marking items as spam, the computer will learn. You may also protect others who are receiving the same messages.

42.   Use a filter program on top of the one that your e-mail service provider gives you. There are a number of good products on the market. Avoid downloading any you have never heard of or are "new," as they could contain spyware. Instead, look for a program made by one of the major companies, like Microsoft®, or look for a product that such a company recommends or sells on their Web site.

43.   Do not "unsubscribe" to spam e-mail. That is just a way to sell your e-mail address to more spam lists. Notice that I have said "spam" and not "bulk." Spam e-mail does go to your bulk folder, but if you sign up for an online newsletter, it might go to your bulk folder along with the spam. This happens because most spam filters mark messages that are sent to large groups of people. If you know you have signed up for an e-mail service, you can unsubscribe without any problems.

44.   If you are receiving a lot of spam, complain to the IP address and ask to be removed. Simply hit the "reply" button and you are well on your way to being off the list. Be polite the first time you e-mail them and remember, it may take a few days or even a week to enter your information allowing you to unsubscribe. However, being polite does not have to mean that you are not firm. Put your foot down and do not take no for an answer. If you have not been unsubscribed in two weeks, e-mail the IP address again and check up on why you are still receiving junk e-mail.

45. If you post messages in forums, do not post your e-mail address. If you really have to post your e-mail address, write it like this: name-at-gmail-dot-com. That way, spam bots will not pick it up as readily. Think twice, though. Do you really need to include your e-mail address? Most forums include a system where users can privately message one another. It is a tiny built-in e-mail system. Check to see that your private mailbox is enabled if you have one. You can even choose to sync it with your regular e-mail. That way, whenever you receive a private message from someone in the forums, you will receive an e-mail alerting you of that message to your regular inbox. That way, you do no even have to remember to check it.

46. Have more than one e-mail account. When you have to sign up for something online, use your "junk" e-mail address. It is fairly simple to sign up for a Yahoo! or Gmail account, and you can use this address to filter out the non-sensitive e-mails you may receive. If you are signing up for an account linked to your credit card, use your regular, secure e-mail. For everything else, use the dummy e-mail.

47. If you have a Web site, give users a form to contact you instead of posting your e-mail address. You can find several free online resources for creating contact forms in any type of Web site design program. You do not have to know HTML well to make this work for you. By using a form, you are avoiding tons of spam e-mail and you can also be sure that the e-mails you do get do not end up in the wrong folder because they had a weird subject line or were sent to multiple people. On top of that, when you use a form, it records the IP address. If there is a problem down the road, having the IP address will really help you solve it or alert you to other fraudulent e-mails.

48.   Give to charities you know and trust. At the very least, avoid giving online. If you get an e-mail about a charity needing help, call them, research them to make sure they are legitimate, and send a check. Remember, though, donating to a specific charity is not necessary to reach the people who are in need. In other words, any charity focusing on Katrina victims will be putting their money in the same place. Therefore, if you are moved to donate to a certain organization but are not sure it is legitimate, look for a different one that you can confirm is doing the same thing. Some "basic" charities that you may want to consider:

- The Red Cross (disaster relief and emergency help)

- Make-a-Wish (terminally ill children)

- The Ronald McDonald House (families with sick children)

- The Heifer Project (world hunger)

- Relay for Life (cancer research)

- Toys for Tots (holiday gifts for needy children)

- Habitat for Humanity (shelter for the homeless)

- Your local Goodwill or Salvation Army

- Any program sponsored by a well-known corporation

- Any college/university giving program

- Your neighborhood school's PTA

- Your local EMT, ambulance, or fire house (especially if they are volunteer-run)

- Your local church, temple, synagogue, or other house of worship

49. Do not assume that a charity is legitimate because it has a legitimate-sounding name. Many scam artists will steal your credit card number using a site that has "Red Cross," "World Trade Center," "Tsunami," or "Katrina" in their domain name. They take advantage of that fact that there are legitimate disaster relief charities helping the cause. As new disasters happen and needs arise, new fake charities begin to launch Web sites. It is a continuous cycle.

50. Contact your state charity-regulating offices to determine that a charity is real before you donate. Every state keeps a running list of nonprofit organizations, as well as contact information and statistics about that organization. You can usually find a number for the state office online at your state's Web site, or you can look in your phone book under "government." If you are not sure what number to call, just call the main office number listed. The switchboard operator will be able to transfer you to the correct person, and that is a lot easier than spending hours looking for an obscure number online.

51. Opt out of all mailing lists, online and offline. Here are the contacts for the major companies that sell mailing lists. Send a letter to each asking that your name be removed:

Mail Preference Service
Direct Marketing Association
PO Box 9008
Farmingdale, NY 11735

Telephone Preference Service
Direct Marketing Association
PO Box 9014
Farmingdale, NY 11735

Database America
Compilation Department
470 Chestnut Ridge Road
Woodcliff, NJ 07677

Dun & Bradstreet
Customer Service
899 Eaton Avenue
Bethlehem, PA 18025

Metromail Corporation
List Maintenance
901 West Bond
Lincoln, NE 68521

R.L. Polk & Co. Name Deletion File
List Compilation Development
26955 Northwestern Highway
Southfield, MI 48034-4716

52.   Keep track of all correspondence when you are attempting to fix a security problem or opting out of services, such as in the case above. Send your mail certified so that you receive a ticket with the name and signature of the person who received it. Print off a copy of all letters – snail mail and e-mail – that you have sent and mark the date. File carefully. Most important of all, if you suspect that something is wrong, record your phone messages. In some places, there are laws that state that certain people or businesses have to tell the caller that they are being recorded. So know the law, but take that crucial step. You may need the conversation for later.

USING YOUR COMPUTER

53. Buy a lock for any bag in which you will be carrying your laptop and keep that bag locked whenever the computer is inside. Most important, do not keep the key in one of the bag's outside pocket. Carry the keys on your person if you can, protecting them like you would a set of car keys. In fact, a good place to keep your keys for your laptop bag is on the key ring with your house keys and car keys. Make a spare and keep it someone safe, like in a fireproof safe or safety deposit box. It may seem like a lot of trouble for just a computer bag key, but you will thank yourself if your bag is ever stolen, which can be done quite easily, especially at an airport.

54. When working on a laptop in a public place, avoid going onto any sites that require a password or PIN. Security cameras can pick up this kind of information, and you can never be sure just how trustworthy those watching the tapes may be. Even if there are no cameras, it is easy for someone to look over your shoulder.

55. If you are working in a public place and must use a site requiring a password, change it as soon as you get home. Do not use a version of the original password; think of something completely different. That way, if anyone did happen to memorize your password or PIN, it will be useless to them by the time they try to use it.

56. Avoid using public computers, such as those found at the library, for signing into any accounts. If you must, make sure you clear the cache before logging offline, and, like noted in the tip before, change your password or PIN when you get home.

57.   When you get rid of your computer, get an expert to make sure that absolutely all the information is wiped from it, even if you do not think that you have stored any sensitive information on it while you had the computer. This is a crucial step even if you are simply throwing the computer away instead of reselling it. The right technicians can repair a broken computer from a dumpster to retrieve data from it.

58.   Never visit a Web site that you would not want others to know you are visiting. You actions on the Internet can and will be traced. This is a good tip to use in your daily life, not just in regards to Internet identity security. Your husband will find out if you have a profile on online dating sites. The police will find out that you are looking at child pornography. The list goes on and on. When in doubt, just do not do it. The Internet is not a secure world.

59.   Never write anything in an e-mail that you would not want others to know you are writing. Again, this can be tracked and intercepted. Besides, you never know when the recipient will have his or her account hacked or password stolen.

60.   Do not open e-mails from senders you do not recognize, especially if they are in your bulk mailbox.

It is better for the sender to have to resend information that you have deleted than to accidentally get sucked into a scam or installing spyware on your computer.

61. Configure your e-mail to prevent anyone from connecting to your SMTP port. This will help protect you from hackers spoofing your e-mail address.

62. Use a password upon start up. Yes, most hackers can get through this rather easily, but every little step helps. This wall of protection might mean the difference of a few hours, giving you time to alert your credit card companies, bank, and other financial institutions that your information may have been compromised. It also means that you will have time to log into your online accounts and change your passwords or lock them completely.

63. Monitor your children's activities online. Children do not often understand that giving out personal information can be detrimental. Remember, though, your child's identity is as much at risk as your own. Talk to your children about identity theft and go over what is acceptable and not acceptable to do online. Keep the conversations age-appropriate, and remember that even the best conversation does not replace a watchful eye.

64. If possible change your computer settings so that your children cannot log on unless you are in the room. Also, look into investing in programs that block the Internet. Today's technology allows you to determine a specific list of sites where your children may visit. All other sites will be locked out. Work out a list of fun and educational sites together. There are a number of great programs that allow you to do this, including the following:

- Crayon Crawler

- Kidsafe Explorer

- Cybersitter

- Netmop

- KidSplorer

- The Bsafe Online Internet Explorer

65. Realize the potential of a good baby-sitter or tutor. If your child needs to use the Internet for a school project but you are too busy taking care of other children, cooking dinner, working, etc. to monitor his or her activities, hire a responsible local college student (or even a mature high school student if your own child is fairly young) to monitor the computer activity.

66. When you are away from your desk at work, even for just a few minutes, log off of your account so that your computer cannot be accessed by anyone else in the office. Even if everyone else is in the same meeting as you, delivery people, interns, and secretaries could still use your computer without you knowing it.

67.   If you are going to be away from your desk at work for any amount of time, do not just log off of your computer – also lock your door. Again, if someone really, really wants to get to your personal account on that computer, they will find a way, but every little step helps. It will take someone longer if they have to pick a lock and then figure out a password, and in that extra time, they could be caught or have to quickly leave because you are coming back to your office.

68.   An Extra-Long Tip: How to Wipe Your Hard Drive

One of the most important tips for helping to protect your identity from online criminals is to wipe your hard drive and delete important files completely. This is a skill that everyone with a computer should know how to do, yet few actually ever learn. Why is it so important? Well, when you delete something from your computer, it is not really gone. Due to the changes in the computer world, information is staying on your computer longer, meaning someone who knows what he or she is doing could still access sensitive items you deleted a few months ago. Wiping your hard drive prevents this access.

So, why does the delete button not actually delete your files? It seems like a lot of work to delete a single file. This characteristic of computers actually comes from a time when computers were very, very slow. It takes a long time to delete files, or rather, it took a long time to delete files (computers now are much faster). So, instead of having a consumer wait forever for a file to delete, the computer just deletes the path to the file, telling the computer that it is all right to overwrite the file when more space is needed. Unless you actually delete the file (not just the path), someone who knows where to look can still recover those files. You cannot search on your computer anymore to find them, but there are back doors to get into these files. Any file you do not fully wipe is at risk, including word-processed documents, pictures, and videos. Eventually, your computer will overwrite these documents, but that could take months or even years since computers have much more memory than they did in the past.

Do not panic. Wiping your hard drive is fast, easy, and free. You do not have to be an expert to learn how this works. Of course, make sure that you really want to delete a file, because you will not be able to get it back, even if you are the smartest, most well-trained computer technician in the world.

To wipe your hard drive, you need a program. These can be a bit tricky to find, even on the Internet. Although you may at first think that wiping programs should be a staple in the computer world, like anti-spyware programs, the government puts pressure on manufacturers to not offer wiping programs. Remember, bad guys use them, too. Imagine how these wipers can be dangerous, for example, when used by someone running a child pornography ring. One call to tip that person off and the entire computer can be wiped before the FBI shows up.

A wiping program deletes a file by overwriting it with gibberish or blank space at least once. For maximum security, you should be able to set the program to overwrite your files multiple times. The more secure you want to be, the longer it will take to run on your computer, so make sure you have plenty of free time to allow the program to do its job. Running it overnight is a good idea.

Start backing up any document or program that you don't want to lose. Like mentioned above, you will absolutely not be able to retrieve this program once you have wiped your computer clean. Common things that people forget to back up include:

- Music

- My Downloads

- Programs that you didn't install with a CD or that you do not have the CD for anymore

- Fonts

- My Favorites

- My Bookmarks

- Pictures

- Plugins

You have a number of options in order to back up the items that you need. All of these options work well, as long as you remember to destroy the copies when you have your computer up and running again if there is sensitive information on them:

- **Use an external hard drive.** This is probably the best option, as you can simply install it on your computer and then drag and drop all of your files into it on a weekly or monthly basis. External hard drives do not have operating systems on them, so you cannot open and use your files on there, but they do effectively store any file, so you can simply reinstall what you want when your computer is wiped clean. Note that you also may want to wipe your external hard drive after you are finished.

- **E-mail your files to yourself.** This is a fairly insecure way to save files so it should not be used to save sensitive information. In addition, you will probably not be able to e-mail huge files to yourself, as there is a limit to the size of your attachments and the size of your inbox. However, it is a good option if you simply want to save a file or two.

- **Burn your information onto CDs.** This is a great way to store things that you will always need and that will remain stagnant. In other words, it isn't a good option for files that you want to edit and back up often, as you cannot continually rewrite a CD and will end up spending a ton of money on blank CDs. However, it is a good way to store things like pictures and music.

- **Use another computer.** If nothing else, you can transfer your files to another computer and store them there until you wipe your hard drive. This is a good option only if you are storing non-sensitive files. Also, remember that your back up computer can crash just as easily as your primary computer, since it has an operating system. This is the least secure way to back up your files, but will work in a pinch.

Next, do a low-level wipe. This will not fully protect your computer, but it is a good start and will keep anyone who does not know much about computers from accessing your sensitive files. If you're using an older version of Windows, you will need to create a start-up disk by following your computer's instructions. However, if you are using Windows XP or later versions, or if you have a Mac, the disk will be included in the packet of disks when you buy your computer. Restart your computer with the disk in the drive and you should get an option to boot from the CD. Follow the instructions on the screen, deleting everything as it pops up, and you'll have a fairly blank slate to start.

There are a number of wiping programs that you can then use to completely wipe your hard drive. Check out the following programs, making sure to read reviews and news before you use anything that supposedly wipes your hard drive. Downloading programs from the Internet, no matter how they are marketed, is always risky, and you do not want to accidentally download a virus that steals your information!

- Total Wipe Pro (cost $19.95)

- WipeDrive (cost $39.95)

- Free Disk Wipe (cost free)

- QuickWiper (cost $29.95)

- Stellar Wipe (cost $39.00)

As of right now, the best on the market for most people is probably WipeDrive. However, because of increasing pressure from law enforcement agencies and the government, wiping program manufacturers were constantly closing up shop, opening under different names, and otherwise becoming available and unavailable. Do your research to find out what programs are available and which ones work the best today at the moment you are reading this book.

OFFLINE PROTECTION

69. Shred your mail, including all credit card offers you may receive. Criminals are not above diving through your dumpster to find information they can use. And believe me: They can use the tiniest piece of information to start their theft of your identity. From credit card offers to old bank statements, you need to shred almost anything you throw away. Shredding is fast and shredders are inexpensive, so there is really no reason not to shred your documents. When in doubt, shred.

70. Watch your mail carefully, because thieves often steal it before you get home. Invest in a mailbox that locks or use a post office box if you do not have a door slot. At the very least, make sure that you get your mail every day. If you usually get a few pieces and have not received mail in a few days, call your post office.

71. Opt out of pre-approved credit card offers, which are often a target for identity thieves. You can opt out fairly easily by calling the Opt Out Request Line at 1-888-567-8688.

72. Never give out personal information over the phone, even if someone can refer to your account number. Instead, tell the caller that you are busy and need to call back in a few minutes. Then, call your bank using their official number or stop at your bank in person. If the call was legitimate, they will be willing to wait for your information.

73. Keep your social security card in a safe place, not in your wallet, which can be stolen fairly easily.

74. Do not include yourself on any of the Who's Who publications. Most professionals are offered this "honor," but it is simply an avenue for people to find out a lot of personal information about you. Opting out will not mean you are any less respectable professionally.

75. Use traveler's checks when on vacation or carry a secured credit card.

76. If your driver's license is issued to include your social security number, call your state department of motor vehicles and ask that it be changed. You may have to pay a fee to get a new license, but it is well worth the money.

77. The same is true for any identification card you carry or wear, including your insurance card, an employee identification card, and so forth. You should never carry your social security number with you unless you specifically need it for some reason.

78. Check your own credit report once a year. You can do this every 12 months without any repercussions. If you see anything suspicious, do not panic — it could simply be a mistake. Call the major credit reporting bureaus right away to find out what is going on.

79. Keep your credit card in sight when using it to pay anything to avoid having someone skim the card and steal the information on it, which means take cash when you pay at a restaurant. Waiters and waitresses are the most common people to steal your credit card information by skimming, because at most restaurants, the cash register is not near your booth or table. Even if it is, you are usually so engrossed with eating and talking to your dinner date that you will have your guard down. Do not be fooled by a friendly server. Keep the card close to you whenever possible, and if you have to use a card to pay for your meal, use a debit or prepaid card. The number on those cards will not do thieves much good since they will not have your PIN.

80.   Sign the back of your card. Experts agree that this is the safest way to protect yourself. Some people like to write "Check ID" on the back, thinking it is safer, but for someone who really wants to steal your identity, it is not hard to make up a fake ID. It is much harder to fake a signature. Or, rather, it is easier to prove that a signature is not yours. Therefore, if your card is stolen and a thief makes purchases, you can look at the store's signature copy and compare it to your own. If it does not match, the store should be willing to take responsibility for the bad purchases. After all, they are supposed to compare signatures right away. It is harder to prove that someone used a fake ID to make purchases, simply because more clerks do not memorize your face after you use your credit card. If the thief looked similar to you, there is a good chance the clerk would not be able to tell you apart in a line up. When nothing out of the ordinary happens, it is hard to remember a face. Think about it; can you picture the face of the last clerk that helped you at a mini mart or checked you out at the grocery store?

81.   Cancel credit cards you do not use. The fewer cards you have, the easier it will be to watch out for suspicious activity. To cancel a credit card, do not just cut it up and throw it away. It is important to actually call the company to have the account closed. Otherwise, the account will still be open for purchases and open to attack, even if you do not carry a balance. On another note, officially closing your credit card account will help improve your credit score and will stop you from paying any kind of annual minimum balance fee, which is required by many major credit cards.

82.   Use a smart card, which is a pre-paid credit card that works like a debit card. Or use a credit card with a fairly low limit. The less the crooks have access to, the better. You can get a smart card from any of the major credit card companies.

83.   Lenders will increase your credit limit all the time, just for paying the card on time or being a cardholder for a certain number of months or years. If you do not need that extra spending money, call and request that your credit limit be lowered. Credit card companies are supposed to notify you when there is a change, but some simply state in the contract that your limit will increase at specific times. Keep track of how much credit you have and how much you really need.

84.   Take your receipt with you when you purchase something with your credit card. Although credit card slips do not show all of your information, giving thieves even a little piece, like your name, signature and the last four numbers, is dangerous.

85.   Only use bank ATMs, not privately-owned ATMs, which are much more likely to have attachments that skim your card and steal information from it. If you really need money and cannot find a bank, use your debit card to pay for purchases at a store like Kmart or Wal-Mart. Most of these stores have a cash-back option and you can use this as an instant, usually free, ATM. It is safer than using a privately owned ATM and usually cheaper, too.

86.   Before using an ATM, be a bit observant. Where is the security camera located? Use your hand to cover the key pad as you type in your pin, just in case an identity thief tapped into the camera's feed. Be aware, however, that it is not a good idea to block the view of the camera in any way. For example, do not hang a hat over the camera to block the view. If a security guard is watching, he or she will think that something suspicious is going on, and depending where you live, such practice may be illegal. You do not actually want to hide your actions when using the ATM, just your PIN number.

87.   Check the ATM for any signs of tampering. If possible, use the same ATM every time you need money, and if you notice any changes, contact your bank. It is possible that the bank upgraded their ATM, but it is also possible that an identity thief added a skimming machine to the card reader.

88.   For financial counseling, accounting matters, and credit counseling, work only with reputable businesses. Counselors should be accredited with the National Foundation for Credit Counseling or the Association of Independent Consumer Credit Counseling Agencies. Before you release sensitive information, you should review the company's confidentiality policy, ask for a list of past clients, and otherwise do a bit of research. Think of it as if you are interviewing an employee. You do not have to use a company just because they have come recommended. Do a bit of investigating to find out who will work best for you.

89.   Do not choose to work with any company solely by surfing the Internet. You should always visit a real life office or, at the very least, do research to pair with telephone conversations. The only exception to this rule would be big companies that are extremely popular and, in some cases, do not have brick-and-mortar offices. Examples of such businesses include ING, PayPal, and eBay. When in doubt, just do not use that Web site. There are plenty of options for anything you want to do.

90.   If you see your social security number being used anywhere, such as on your health insurance card or employee identification, talk to the customer service department about changing this information. Make sure you check out all your accounts, including loans, credit cards, and so forth.

91.   Use an assumed name when possible, which is totally legal as long as you have no intent to deceive. A good idea is to use your middle name or initials for your everyday communications. Only use your real, full name when you need to use it, such as with the police or with the government.

92. Ask to update your medical information whenever you go in for your annual check up. Make sure your medical records are not showing any weird visits, treatments, or prescriptions that you do not remember.

93. Find out how your information is stored professionally. You should ask your doctor, accountant, and lawyer at the very least for information about protection procedures and how they are watching for identity theft. There are thousands of professionals in every state, so if you feel like yours are not doing enough to keep you safe, take your business elsewhere.

94. If you are self-employed, apply for a separate tax identification number, called an EIN. This is what you should use in place of any form that requires your social security number, including your income taxes. Traditionally, EINs are used for employee purposes, but you can apply for and receive an EIN even if you do not have any employees.

95. An Extra-Long Tip: Learning about Identity Theft Laws

If knowledge truly is power in the identity theft prevention world, then learning about just how you are protected is key. While there are a number of laws pertaining to identity theft, there are still many loopholes that identity thieves are using to overcome the law. You can help stop them by writing to your local and state government to propose change. New identity theft bills, both protecting people online and offline, are being proposed every day to help prevent, catch, and punish criminals. Doing your part can help make the world safer fro everyone. Learn about the following laws:

96.   The Fair Credit Reporting Act: Under the Fair Credit Reporting Act, consumer reporting agencies are allowed to collect and distribute your personal information. However, they must do so fairly and with your security in mind. First, these agencies must take steps to verify information and resolve disputers. If information is taken off due a disputer, the consumer must be notified if it is put back on the report. In addition, negative information can only be reported for seven years (with the exception of bankruptcy, which can be reported for ten years).

Also under this law, information furnishers (ie, creditors who report your activity with their company) must provide complete and accurate information, investigate any and all disputes, and inform customers when negative information is to be reported on your account.

If anyone uses your report for anything (say, for instance, to raise your interest rate because your credit score has dropped), they must notify you of the adverse action they are about to take. They must also give you the name of the company that provided your credit report so that you can investigate anything you believe is incorrect.

All of these actions are to protect you from going through life without knowing that your credit score is falling. Since you are notified, you can catch errors and dispute things that were caused by identity thieves. If these laws were not in effect, you might go years without knowing that your credit score is falling. That gives the identity thieves only a few months to get away before you know something is wrong, rather than being about to ruin your credit for many years.

97.   The Fair Credit Billing Act: This act protects your credit score when there are errors on your billing statements, which is often the case if an identity thief steals your credit card. Until the matter is resolved, the following things must be kept from your credit report:

- Charges not made by you

- Damaged goods

- Billing errors doing to wrong calculations

- Goods that were never delivered

- Statements mailed to the wrong address

- Charges that were never made

You must send written notice that you are disputing something in order for these laws to protect you.

98. Electronic Funds Transfer Act: Because so many of us use our credit and debt cards to purchase things online, and because even more people do online banking, the Electronic Funds Transfer Act is great for protecting consumers, merchants, and lenders dealing with identity theft. The consumer must:

- Contact the lender within 60 days of the error on the statement

- Release name and account number

- Fully explain why the charge is erroneous

- Send details of the dispute in writing within 10 business days, if requested by the lender.

At the same time, the lender must:

- Investigate and attempt to resolve the dispute within 45 days, or within 90 days if it involved the erroneous opening of a new account

- Recredit any amounts found to be incorrect

- Notify the customer if they catch an error

- Explain findings that were deemed not to be erroneous

- Send copies of any documents used in the investigation at the consumer's request.

In addition, the Electronic Funds Transfer Act helps to determine who is liable for faulty charges in the case of a lost or stolen card:

- If your card is lost or stolen and you report it before any charges have been made, you are not liable for any charges made to that card.

- If your card is lost or stolen and a charge is made, you are liable for $50 worth of charges if you report the loss within 2 business days.

- If your card is lost or stolen and you report it as such after 2 business days, but within 60 business days, you are responsible for charges up to $500.

- If your card is lost or stolen and you do not report it within 60 business days, you could be liable for all charges made to that account.

Unfortunately, they vary a bit from state to state, but if you reference the following documents in your local courthouse or online, you should be able to find the exact laws that pertain to you and other citizens in the state where you live:

Alabama: Alabama Code 13A-8 -190 through 201

Alaska: Alaska Statutes Title 11, Chapter 46, Section 565

Arizona: Arizona Rev. Statute 13-2008

Arkansas: Arkansas Code 5-37-227

California: California Penal Code 530.5-8

Colorado: Colorado Article 5, 18-5-901, Part 9

Connecticut: Connecticut Statute 53a-129a and 52-571h

Delaware: Delaware Code Title II, 854

District of Columbia: District of Columbia 22-3227

Florida: Florida Statute 817.568

Georgia: Georgia Code Title 16, Chapter 9, Article 8

Hawaii: Hawaii Statute 708-839-6 through 8

Idaho: Idaho Code 18-3126

Illinois: 720 Illinois Statute 5-16 G

Indiana: Indiana Code 35-43-503.5

Iowa: Iowa Code 715A8 and Iowa Code 714.16B

Kansas: Kansas Statute 21-4018

Kentucky: Kentucky Statute 514.160

Louisiana: Louisiana. Rev. Statute 14:67.16

Maine: Maine Rev. Statute 17-A 905-A

Maryland: Maryland. Code Article 27-231

Massachusetts: Massachusetts General Laws Chapter 266, 37E

Michigan: Michigan Laws 750.285

Minnesota: Minnesota. Statute 609.527

Mississippi: Mississippi Code 97-19-85

Missouri: Missouri Statute 570.223

Montana: Montana Code 45-6-332

Nebraska: Nebraska Statute 28-608 and 28-620

Nevada: Nevada Statute 205.463-465

New Hampshire: New Hampshire Statute 638:26

New Jersey: New Jersey Statute 2C:21-17

New Mexico: New Mexico Statute 30-16-24.1

New York: New York Penal Code 190.77 through 190.84

North Carolina: North Carolina General Statute 14-113.20-23

North Dakota: North Dakota Code 12.1-23-11

Ohio: Ohio Code 2913.49

Oklahoma: Oklahoma Statute Title 21, 1533.1

Oregon: Oregon Statute 165.800

Pennsylvania: 18 Pennsylvania Constitutional State 4120

Rhode Island: Rhode Island General Laws 11-49.1-1

South Carolina: South Carolina Code 16-13-500, 501

South Dakota: South Dakota Codified Laws 22-30A-3.1

Tennessee: Tennessee 39-14-150 and Tennessee 47-18-2101

Texas: Texas Penal Code 32.51

Utah: Utah Code 76-6-1101-1104

Vermont: Vermont State Code 13-2030

Virginia: Virginia Code 18.2-186.3

Washington: Washington Code 9.35.020

West Virginia: West Virginia Code 61-3-54

Wisconsin: Wisconsin Statute 943.201

Wyoming: Wyoming Statute 6-3-901

5

A NOTE ABOUT LIVING ANONYMOUSLY

Preventing online identity theft really only requires a few simple changes to your everyday life. In other words, to stay safe, you do not have to go into the witness protection program. There is really no excuse, then, to not protect yourself and your finances from identity theft. Living anonymously, however, is a whole other story.

A person may want to live anonymously for a number of reasons. Some people are trying to prevent a certain someone from finding them. Others have identities that can really be used for evil if stolen (think secret service agents or the like). Maybe you simply like your privacy. In any case, living anonymously is by far the best way to stop identity theft. After all, "anonymous" means that you barely have an identity at all. To totally live beneath the radar, however, you need to make really big changes in your life. Not everyone can successfully do the following, but they are tips you should consider if you want to take your prevention measures, online and offline, to the next level.

AN ALTERNATIVE IDENTITY

Alternative identities — it may seem like something right out of a James Bond movie, but in reality, using an alternative identity is very, very smart. It makes it more difficult to "see" you on paper, making it virtually impossible for something to steal your identity. Best of all, it is perfectly within your rights to take on an alternative identity, as long as you are not doing so with the intent to defraud a person, business, or government agency. You have the right to be whoever you want to be. People choose to live with alternative identities all the time. In addition to helping you avoid identity theft, an alternative identity can also help people leave behind abusive relationships, forget a past full of mistakes, avoid civil lawsuits, leave their families, and otherwise just disappear. While this can be extremely frustrating for someone trying to find you, it might be in your best interest.

The key to an alternative identity is to ensure that your real name and pretend name are never linked. Legally, you are allowed to create any kind of official-looking document you want to "confirm" your alternative name against, as long as you are not doing so with the intent to defraud anyone. For example, if you have decided to take on the identity of a retired doctor, you can create a fake license with your alternative name on it, print it off, and hang it in your office for anyone in your home to see — just do not try to practice medicine with it.

Some Fun: Celebrity Alternative Identities

One of the best uses of alternative identities is for celebrities. In fact, a good number of celebrities have a stage name and almost every celebrity in the world has given a fake name at a hotel at some point or another. That is the only real way to keep the paparazzi and crazy fans from infiltrating your travel and your family life (and even then it sometimes does not work).

Just for fun, can you guess the "celebrity" name of the following people? The answers can be found in Appendix 3.

1. Norman Cook

2. Ferdinand Lewis Alcindor Jr.

3. Erica Wright

4. Kong-Sang Chan

5. Brian Warner

6. Alissa Rosenbaum

7. Theodore Geisel

8. Robert Edward Turner III

9. Marion Michael Morrison

10. Robert Cummings

And how about this – can you name the real celebrity that has previously given these fake names at hotels and other places to avoid fans and photographers? The answers can be found in Appendix 4.

1. Miss Lollipop

2. Tinkerbell

3. Bella

4. Arnold Schwarzenegger

5. Sir William Marshal

6. Johnny Drama

7. Mr. Satan

8. Emma Roid

9. Sir Galahad

10. Bryce Pilaf

The bottom line? Using a fake name is not a crime, as long as you are not trying to outrun the law. Celebrities do it all the time, and there is no reason why you cannot do it too, in most cases!

Where You Can and Cannot Use an Alternative Name

The bottom line when using an alternative name is that you have to know the laws where you live. Having an alternative identification for protection purposes is not a crime. In fact, the government runs a program that helps people do just that. Every day, people in danger disappear using the Witness Protection Program. The key here? The government still knows who you are. Your newfound friends do not have to know your real name, but you should never try to fool the government. Doing so can — and will — end with you in jail or, at the very least, paying some hefty fines.

Most people volunteer personal information at the drop of a hat. Why do you have to use your name to register your computer, for example? What about when you sign up for an online e-mail account? Or, for example, when the girl at the coffee counter asks for your name to write it on your coffee cup, why do you have to tell her? There is nothing wrong with giving an alternative name. Think of it as a nickname.

Again, it depends on your state's laws — but a good way to think about it is by asking yourself if the information is for official purposes of not. Few transactions on a daily basis are actually "official." When you open a bank account, it is official business. When you apply for a mortgage, it is official business. When an officer pulls you over for speeding, it is official business. However, when your neighbor asks for your name and number so she can call you if there is ever a noise problem? That is not official business.

ANONYMOUS RESIDENCES

The first step to living anonymously is finding a place to actually live. Your residence will be, in most cases, the one thing tied to your name, even if the name you give is an alternative one. People will associate your face with the place that you live. There is no getting around that.

What you can "get around" is being associated with bills, as well as accounts, in your name. You can also learn techniques for moving quickly and often, as well as the safest ways to stay out of the public eye. You may not be a celebrity, but that is what living anonymously is all about – the "public eye". When the public does not know much about you, neither can identity thieves, or anyone trying to find you for that matter.

When it comes to place of residence, you have two main options: renting or owning. If you have the means, you can also choose to stay in a hotel, which is actually a form of renting when you think about it. Both renting and owning have their drawbacks, but consider both carefully to decide which one is right for you.

Staying in Hotels

Although it is definitely the most expensive option and does not make a lot of sense if you are trying to build a financial portfolio, staying in a hotel is probably the least intrusive way to live. You do not have to give your real name. You do not have to pay for utilities. However, it does mean that you have to pare down the possessions you own, since you will be moving often. For those who live a simple life, though, staying in hotels could work.

Your best bet for saving money and not raising suspicion is to look for extended stay suites. These suites are miniature apartments, and although they are more expensive than regular apartments, they come fully furnished and with all of the services you'll find in a typical hotel room. Extended stay suites are commonly used by people who are in town on business for a month or more or for people who are just moving into an area and need time to hunt for a conventional place of residence. Why are you staying there? They should not ask and you should not have to answer that question.

When you get to the hotel, they will want to see identification, as well as have a card on file in case there are damages to the room. You are well within your rights to use a prepaid credit card that is held in your alternative name, as well as give a novelty ID with your alternative name and a picture. They will most likely make a photocopy of your ID, and you wouldn't want to give them your driver's license in this case.

In addition, the hotel will want to keep your vehicle information on record. Renting a car is a good idea to avoid this link to your real name, or you can register a car in the name of a trust. Having a trust fund set up and using this name when needed is an excellent way to avoid linking your name to your alternative name or your location.

For the most privacy, however, stay in a low-end motel – just do not expect the same services you would find at the Hilton. Low-end motels have many customers who rent just for a night and do not wish to be tracked, so some do not even require you to keep a card on file or to show identification.

Renting and Owning

If you do not want to be as mobile as someone living from a hotel, renting is your next best option. You can acquire more things than you can in a hotel room, and you do not have to deal with people coming into your room, as maids do in hotels. There are, of course, a number of disadvantages, but for more people wishing to live anonymously, renting works very well. It is much easier than owning and trying to live anonymously.

First, consider your length of stay. Most people living anonymously like to be able to move fairly quickly, which is only possible if you are renting. If you buy and own a property, you and your name are linked to it even if you move out of the area quickly. You have to sell the house, which requires you to stay linked to that property for a fairly long time. When renting, you will be able to find many lease options. Although the majority of landlords ask you to sign a one-year lease, you can find many who will agree to much shorter 3-month or 6-month leases. You can even find landlords willing to rent to you on a month-to-month basis.

Another major benefit is that all work that needs to be done and all ownership is in your landlord's name, not in your name. If you own a house, you'll have to pay quite a number of bills, including carpenters and other maintenance people, unless you are extremely handy and can do the work yourself. In addition, there will be no property taxes in your name. Property tax documents are places where it is illegal to give an alternative name, since you are dealing with the federal and state governments. Therefore, if you want to avoid that link to your name, renting is the way to go.

Furthermore, when renting, you do not have to deal with a mortgage. If you can afford to purchase a house in cash, that is wonderful. However, for most people, that is just a dream and a mortgage is necessary to purchase a piece of real estate. A mortgage is yet another tie to your name, and although you can use a trustee to sign for you, it is a much better option to simply forego the property ownership altogether. Not to mention that a mortgage will make it next to impossible to leave the area quickly if you feel like your identity has been compromised. Even if you do not financially need to sell your home to move on, you will still need to pay your mortgage.

Utilities

With utilities, you must have real name connected, because this information can be reported on your credit. That said, no one said that it has to be your name found on the utility bills. There are a number of ways to get around that fence.

First, look for an apartment that has utilities included. In many cases, you can find some that include the basics – gas, electric, water, sewer, and trash. You may even get lucky and find one that includes cable TV and Internet. This is most common in areas with high student populations. However, if these things are NOT included, talk to your landlord about including them. Find out how much cable and Internet will cost every month and then offer more if your landlord has it set up before you move in. For example, if it will cost $75 a month, offer your landlord an additional $100 to take care of it. Most will jump at the chance.

If this is not possible, you can use what is called a nominee to set up account on your behalf. A nominee is simply someone you trust and who trusts you and, if the case of living anonymously, should not be a close friend or relative. Look at this as a business interaction. The nominee sets up the account in his or her name and pays it, and you are responsible for paying him or her. Again, it is important that you trust one another and it is important that this person is not closely connected to you so that no links can be made.

Getting to Know the Neighbors

The biggest threat to living absolutely anywhere, whether you rent or whether you own, is getting to know your neighbors. Neighbors always have been and always will be nosy. If nothing else, you'll have neighbors who are friendly and want to get to know you, which is where the problems really begin. In addition, your landlord will want to get to know you in many cases, which can create problems.

You can minimize problems with neighbors by choosing your neighborhood wisely. In an up-scale neighborhood, you will find nicer apartments. Landlords will want to run credit checks and will be adamant about having references. Your neighbors will also be more likely to want to know you, as they will want to make sure that the neighborhood will remain a good place to live. This kind of a neighborhood, although you'll find nice housing, is probably not the best place to live.

On the other hand, a poorer neighborhood you will find an entirely new set of problems – the police. Crime is simply more common in poor neighborhoods, so it is likely that the police will patrol the area regularly. While your neighbors are more likely to keep to themselves, the police like to know exactly who moves into apartments in these areas. In fact, them may try to gather all sorts of information about you, even though you have done nothing wrong. This is also not the kind of neighborhood where you want to live in most cases.

The best neighborhood is somewhere in between. Look for a neighborhood that is off the beaten path but that has a large percentage of apartments for rent. These landlords know that there is a lot of competition, so they are more likely to forego the credit check. This is especially true if you find an area where many of the tenants are immigrants who have no credit to check. If you can pay in full, you are golden. These landlords are also most willing to agree to a month-to-month lease.

When interacting with neighbors, the key is to be the person everyone forgets lives there. Be cordial and friendly, but be private. You can be a good neighbor without offering to baby-sit kids for the girl across the street. Do not cause trouble – clear your sidewalks when it snows, pick up trash that is in your yard, and keep your house looking tidy. That way, no one has any reason to complain about you. At the same time, do not complain about anyone else. If neighbors are loud or unruly either learn to live with it or move. Do not call the police and have your name – even your alternative name – unnecessarily on a police report.

KEEPING YOUR COMMUNICATIONS UNDER WRAPS

It is hard to survive without a telephone. Oh sure, you can do it. Millions of people around the world do not have a telephone in their home. However, in the United States, having a phone is your connection to all sorts of help when you need it. Even if you do not use your phone to chat with friends, you still need a phone to call 9-1-1, talk to creditors, and so forth. Without a phone number, some people will not even consider renting you a place to stay. They want to be able to contact you when they need to.

And then there is e-mail. Now, there are plenty of people who do not have the Internet. However, using e-mail is one of the fastest and easiest ways to contact others, since most businesses, at the very least, have an email address that is checked regularly.

In short, communication is important. Without it, we could not progress as a society. However, if you're attempting to live as anonymously as possible, how do you keep your communication on the down low?

Your Telephone

The first, and easiest, thing you can do to keep your communication private is to un-list your telephone number. You are not legally required to keep your number listed in the phone book, and asking for it to be removed is a simple step that you can – and should – do right away.

Keep in mind, though, that unlisted phone numbers are not much more secure than listed ones. Just because it is not in the phone book does not mean it is not listed anywhere. If you have ever left a number so someone – anyone – can call you back, your phone number is no longer private. Say, for example, that you left your number with a potential apartment manager so that he or she could call you back about a unit for rent. Perhaps he or she then wrote it down along with a few other bits of information about you in order to run a preliminary credit check. That associates your name with a number in the credit reporting bureau's database. From there, it is not hard for your number to find it is way online. The chain continues until your number is no longer private.

Identity thieves who really want to find you can also use a tried and true method – *69. Pressing *69 will give you the callback number if possible. If not, it connects you to an operator who is not supposed to give out your number. "Supposed to" is the key phrase here. A smooth-talking identity thief can, nine times out of ten, convince someone to give up your number. After all, what is it to them?

A better option than a landline is a stand-alone voicemail service. For just a small price every month, you can order a mailbox that is not connected to your name or phone number. This is a great way to ensure that people can reach you. You can then call back on a payphone, cell phone, etc. and not have to worry about your calls being traced to you.

Speaking of cell phones – how secure are they? Not very. However, there are some major benefits to getting a cell phone over getting a landline. First, realize the cell phone's limitations. Your conversations are not secure, as the waves can be picked up by other people and their cell phones as well. Although this does not happen as often as it did in the past, it is still possible. Never give out secure information over the phone. Also, remember that to sign on with a traditional cell phone company, you have to give them lots of information, including your social security number, since you are opening an account. This is very dangerous.

Instead, opt for a prepaid cell phone, like those provided by TracFone. With these phones, which can be purchased by anyone, you do not have to provide any personal information. In fact, all you have to do is purchase the physical phone itself and activate it. If they ask for a name, you are more than welcome to give them your alternative name. Purchase a card with minutes at the store with cash, activate it, and you're ready to make calls.

With any cell phone you choose, remember that criminals can trace it if you have it turned on. It is still in your best interest to have a voicemail service and to only turn on your cell phone if you need to make a call.

Your E-mail

If you are truly trying to live the totally private lifestyle, having an e-mail address at all is probably a bad idea.

However, for many people this is not an option – an e-mail address is needed to contact others. Luckily, e-mail has come a long way in the past few years and is beginning to be more secure.

The least secure e-mail services are those that are free. You will get little customer support and some even sell the information to a third party, which means that you will instantly begin getting spam. These e-mail services are also easiest to hack into. However, paying for e-mail services is not much better. After all, that means that you have to link your credit card information to an e-mail account. This can also be very dangerous.

There are e-mail services that specifically work to keep you protected. HushMail (**www.hushmail.com**) is probably the most well-known service, but there are others as well, some of which are free and some of which are paid. Check out these options, and whatever e-mail you choose to use, pick a very good password and change it often.

FINANCES AND BANKING ON THE DOWN LOW

If you have to do any kind of banking (and who does not have to do banking), you should take special measure to keep your information private, especially if you want to live as anonymously as possible. The best way to do this is a trust account.

Of course, it is possible to live without a bank account. You can very easily use money orders to pay for things or you can go to brick-and-mortar locations and pay in cash (as long as you get a receipt). For most people, though, this is not practical. So, trusts are the way to go.

Experts agree – a trust is the most private form of account you can open. This is due to the fact that there are few regulations saying what does and does not have to be listed in accordance with the trust.

Trusts work a bit differently with every single financial institution, so call around to learn about requirements before you show up in person to apply. Make sure that whatever trust name you choose, it is not even remotely related to your real name or even your alternative name. This trust name can then be used with a debit card and to pay bills.

You can also use a nominee in order to open bank accounts. However, in regards to identity theft, while this is a very private way to keep your account, it also puts you at risk because the nominee has complete legal control over your account. So, if your nominee takes everything, you have no case, even if you do take it to court. You have few rights, and even the most trusted person can be tempted to take large amounts of money. It is in your best interest to use a trust account instead of a nominee, since anyone you trust enough to be a nominee is probably too close to you to be effective and anyone not connected to you is probably someone you do not know well enough to trust.

Make sure that you monitor your financial statements, credit statements, and postal mail. Keeping a close eye on these can easily let you know if you have been the victim of identity theft.

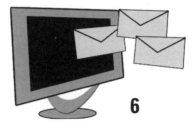

6

HELP! MY IDENTITY WAS STOLEN

Having your identity stolen is devastating, both financially and emotionally. Unfortunately, no matter how many precautions you take to stop identity thieves, they are smart enough to disappear into the woodwork — and, in the process, steal your identity. Once you find out that your identity was stolen, how you react means everything. If you panic, you will only do more damage to yourself and your credit. Keep your cool and work quickly to begin the repair.

WARNING SIGNS THAT YOUR IDENTITY IS IN TROUBLE

If you are proactive, the warning signs that your identity is stolen should be very easy to spot – your credit score will suddenly drop or your credit cards will suddenly be maxed out. Well, in most cases – there are many different kinds of identity theft, remember. So, even if you follow all of the prevention tips listed in this book, you could still be at risk, and you might go weeks or months (or even years) without realizing it. In addition to noticing and following up on anything suspicious you see in your financial accounts, look for the following warning signs of identity theft:

- You do not get a bill or account statement as you normally do. This may mean that someone is having your mail forwarded to them to avoid you catching any mistakes on your account.

- A collection agency contacts you about an account that you do not have – it may not even be in your name.

- You apply for credit and are denied, even though you thought your credit was excellent. Always get a reason if you are denied.

- Your credit card is rejected when you try to make a purchase, even though you know you had enough balance to cover your purchases.

- You suddenly begin getting an abnormal number of e-mails, most of them spam or phishing in nature.

- Someone has tampered with your garbage. They may have been "dumpster diving" – a popular offline way to steal identities.

- You notice personal information about yourself being posted on the Internet.

- Here is one that you need to consider if you have children – your child should not be receiving junk mail. A company should not spend the time or money sending someone who is not 18 information about stuff for which they cannot apply. It is a sign that someone is taking advantage of your child's identity.

HOW TO READ YOUR CREDIT REPORT

Experts agree — once a year you should get a copy of your own credit history report. Checking your credit is not difficult. You can do it online for free by visiting the Web sites of the three major credit-reporting bureaus or you can go to a catch-all site like **www.annualcreditreport. com**, where you can find all three. Usually, if there is a mistake on one due to your identity being stolen, there will be a mistake on all three, but this is not always the case. It really depends on your situation. In any case, there are three major credit reporters – Experian, TransUnion, and Equifax, and all three have credit reporting systems that look very similar. Once you order your free credit report, however, you may have trouble understanding what it means. Credit is reported in certain ways to make the process most efficient for people who really need the information, like lenders. You do not need a decoder ring to understand it, too — simply learn a bit about credit reports and you will be well on your way to catching anything out of the ordinary.

Breaking Down the Credit Report

Every credit report is broken into four major sections to help you find information more easily. For someone who does not know how to read a credit report, the information may seem hidden in a weird place, but in actuality, this sectioning process makes everything uniform and easier to find.

First, you will see a section called identifying information. In this section of the credit report, you will find just that — information that identifies you. This is crucial because there are millions and millions of people in the United States. There are bound to be a few people who have the same name as you and maybe even a few people who have the same birthday. Before you begin panicking about loans you did not know you had, check to ensure that the report is really yours.

Information found in the first section includes your name, your current address, past addresses, your birthday, any telephone numbers associated with you now or in the past, your driver's license number or state ID number, the name of your spouse, the name of your current employers, and your social security number. All the correct information should be listed first. However, be aware that incorrect variations may also be listed. This is especially common if you have a name that is hard to spell or if you have moved often in the past. When information is reported incorrectly, the variations stick with your credit report. It is easier to follow up on a dispute about the variations if they are still listed than it is if they have been deleted. Do not worry about the variations. That does not mean that there will be any mistakes on your credit history report. A red flag you should go up if there are incorrect variations and if you see something that is obviously very wrong. For example, if your name is Michael Jones and a variation is listed as David Johnson, you may want to question it.

Next, you will find a section called "credit history," which is made up of all the individual accounts you have ever opened. These accounts are known as trade lines. For each trade line, you will see listed the date you opened the account, the name or names on the account, the total amount of the loan or credit limit, how much you currently owe, the amount you pay every month if applicable, the type of loan (installments, which will be paid off eventually, or revolving, which is a continuous line of credit), and the status of the account (open, paid, closed, or inactive). There will also be a record of how well you have repaid the loan every month. If you have paid on time and in full, you will see a better rating obviously, but even if you only skipped one payment a year and a half ago, it will still show up as a blemish on your credit history report.

The third section on your credit history report is called "public records." Best-case scenario, this section will be blank. If there is information, it means that you have had financially related problems with the law or government in the past. It will not list criminal activities, but it will list bankruptcies, foreclosures, tax liens, and other judgments against you.

Finally, there will be a section called inquiries. An inquiry is a request to see your credit report, and having too many inquiries may mean that your credit score lowers. There are two kinds of inquiries — hard and soft. Soft inquiries are those done by pre-approved credit cards or other things that you have not personally applied for. They do not really have a bearing on your credit score, and your one personal credit check counts as a soft inquiry once a year. A hard inquiry indicates any credit check that you initiated, such as when you apply for a loan or open a new credit card account. Too many hard inquiries will lower your score because it means that you are attempting to take out lots of loans at once or that you have been turned down by many lenders and have had to apply again and again.

Decoding the Credit Code

In addition to separating the credit report into four organized sections, the credit bureaus also use different codes to more concisely fit everything onto the report. These codes are found in the second section where your accounts are listed. The exact codes used may differ from report to report depending on the agency, but in general, here are the letters of significance:

- I: This is an individual account that is under your sole responsibility.

- J: The account is a joint account, usually between a husband and wife or business partners.

- A: You are an authorized user of the account, but are not responsible for paying it. This is most common when a parent gives a child access to his or her credit card.

- U: The account is undesignated.

- M: You were the maker of the account.

- T: The account has been terminated.

- C: You are the co-signer or the co-maker of the account.

- S: The account is shared.

Under "status" you may see a word or letter, depending on the reporting agency. You will often also see a number ranging from 0 to 9. Here is what they mean:

- O: The account is open.

- R: The account is revolving. That means that it is not a loan that you are working to repay. It is a line of credit that you repay bit by bit, like a credit card.

- I: The account is paid in installments.

- 0: The account is too new to rate in any way.

- 1: You have paid or are paying the account as agreed.

- 2: You are one or two payments behind.

- 3: You are three payments behind.

- 4: You are four payments behind.

- 5: You are more than four payments or 120 days behind.

- 7: Regular payments are being made, but only under taxing your wages.

- 8: A repossession occurred.

- 9: The debt is being actively investigated by a collections agency or court.

Each credit bureau also has codes for describing other aspects, but these vary from union to union. You are likely to find codes for inactive accounts, lost or stolen credit cards, refinanced loans, deaths, foreclosure, bankruptcy, adjustments, and more. Luckily, when you order a credit report, the key for these codes should also be made available to you. Make sure you understand exactly what you are reading, and if anything seems fishy, do not hesitate to call with your questions. That is their job — making sure that your credit is reported correctly. In the case of an identity theft, you may need a lot of help to fix your credit reports.

WHO TO CONTACT

As soon as you suspect that your identity is at risk, it is important to make it well-known. However, most people have no idea who to contact and what to do. The key is to avoid panicking. By thinking clearly and quickly contacting the following people, you can make sure that identity thieves are stopping in their tracks. It may to too late to prevent identity theft, but you do not have to sit back and just let it happen to you. Take action to catch the bad guys.

Credit Reporting Bureaus

If you suspect identity theft for any reason, your first step is to confirm it. Occasionally, there are simply are mistakes that have not resulted from identity theft. The best way to confirm that your identity has been stolen is to contact the major credit reporting companies and get a copy of your credit report. You can also place a fraud flag on your reports and, if you live in certain states, you can "freeze" your account until the matter is cleared.

Equifax
PO Box 740241
Atlanta, GA 30374

1-800-525-6285
www.equifax.com

Experian
Consumer Fraud Assistance
PO Box 9532
Allen, TX 75013
1-888-397-3742
www.experian.com

TransUnion
Fraud Victim Assistance Division
PO Box 6790
Fullerton, CA 92834
1-800-680-7289
www.transunion.com

The Authorities

It is easy to forget that identity theft is a really serious crime, since no one is pointing a gun at you or breaking into your house. Keep this in mind at all times – identity theft is one of the most serious crimes in the world. Who better to contact to report a crime than the police?

Start by reporting the identity theft to your local police in the area where you live, as the crime most likely took place in your neighborhood. Your local police may not be able to help you clear up many of the problems, as there is a limit as to what they can do. However, what they can do, which is very important, is issue a report documenting the identity theft. It is crucial to have this documentation when you try to prove to creditors that your identity really was stolen.

You should also contact the authorities in any place related to the identity theft. This may mean contacting dozens of different police stations, but it is important to do so and to have a copy of the police report mailed to you for each one. Check out where the faulty charges occurred. If the criminal took your credit card and drove to the next state to make charges, you need to call the police in that area to report the problem.

For each police report issued, talk to the police in person or directly on the telephone and get the name and contact information of the person who issued the report. This information will be necessary later when proving your innocence. It is also good to have a record of anyone who helped to catch the criminal in the chance that he or she is caught and the case goes to court.

Creditors

When you find out that your identity has been compromised, you will have the overwhelming urge to yell at anyone involved. However, remember that the creditors are victims in this situation as well. Try as they might, the identity thief will most likely never be caught, which means that they will not be able to recover some of the money they are out from the fraudulent sales or loans. Creditors are on your side.

First, contact any creditor that is showing up as new on your credit history report. This will happen when the thief opens new accounts in your name, takes out loans in your name, and so forth. According to the Fair Credit Reporting Act, a creditor cannot report and fraudulent activity that occurred in your name without your knowledge. Note that you will have to prove that your identity really was stolen, which usually means having the police report, as well as a dispute claim.

You also need to contact all of your current creditors, whether or not they have been affected by the identity theft. Everyone needs to be made aware that your identity was stolen and that everything is a mess at the moment. Some creditors, like a creditor card company, may be directly affected by the crime because the thief used your credit card. Contract these companies first. Other creditors, like your mortgage company, may have floated through the mess untouched. However, when you are done contacting the affected companies, you need to contact the rest as well. Let them know why your interest rate has dropped so significantly and why your credit history report is frozen or flagged. Keeping them "in the know" now can help prevent unnecessary confusion later.

The Federal Trade Commission

Sharing your identity theft experience with the Federal Trade Commission is one of the best ways to help catch identity thieves – perhaps even the one that personally attacked you. The Federal Trade Commission will contact the local authorities handling your case and share valuable information, especially if the case is high-profile or a link in a long chain of crimes by the same person.

In addition, the Federal Trade Commission can help investigate the policies that made your identity theft possible. It is not always an issue with something that you have done to make your identity and personal information susceptible. If a merchant or creditor is putting your information at risk, which is often the case, the Federal Trade Commission can investigate their policies and force changes so that other people do not experience similar identity messes.

With a complaint report from the Federal Trade Commission, you can also put more weight on your situation. When reporting your identity theft to creditors, you have to actually prove that there is a problem. Otherwise, people would buy expensive items and claim identity theft all of the time, just to get out of paying for things! Although having a dispute claim should help to prove your case, by going a step farther and actually registering the problem with the Federal Trade Commission, you can lend more credibility to your situation.

To contact the Federal Trade Commission:

Identity Theft Clearinghouse
Federal Trade Commission

600 Pennsylvania Avenue, NW
Washington, DC 20580
1-877-438-4338

Complaint form: **https://rn.ftc.gov/pls/dod/widtpubl$.
startup?Z_ORG_CODE=PU03**

OTHER IMPORTANT STEPS TO TAKE

Dealing with identity theft is a lot of work. That's the most major downfall. Although you may have identity theft insurance or protection with your accounts to pay for fraudulent charges, it still takes hours and hours of time over the course of many weeks, or even months, to clear up the problems. After you have contacted the appropriate people, make sure that you take the following steps as well.

Close Accounts That Have Been Compromised

When you contact your accounts, especially credit cards, you should freeze them until the matter is cleared up. However, if you unfreeze the cards and continue using them, the identity thief still has relevant information about that account and can attack again or, worse yet, sell that information to the next person who can launch and entirely new attack from someone else in the country – or world!

After you and your credit card company have resolved any disputes surrounding your credit card account (or bank account, or whatever kind of account you have opened), ask both over the phone and in writing that the account be closed. Keep a record of this communication. Ask also that they send you written notification that your account has been closed and all charges have been resolved. File this communication so that it cannot come back to haunt you in the future.

You may then choose to open new accounts. Make sure that these new accounts are not linked in any way to your old, attacked account. You may, in fact, wish to open accounts with another credit card company altogether, which is the safest option. However, wait until all issues with the identity theft are resolved before you apply for a new card. Otherwise, you may find that your interest rate is extremely high due to your falsely inflated credit score.

Consider Getting a New Credit Card

If your identity has really been abused, you may wish to obtain a new Social Security number. However, the Social Security Administration does not hand out new numbers lightly. If they did, people would not protect their Social Security number at all; they would be disposable. Eventually, the numbers would run out and need to be reused, which opens a Pandora's box. That said, if your Social Security number has been involved in a high-scale identity theft crime, you should apply for a new one. Here is how to go about doing it:

1. Download a copy of the application to get the new

Social Security number. You can find applications online at www.ssa.gov.

2. Provide proof that you are a U.S. citizen by providing your birth certificate or immigration papers.

3. Prove that you are who you say you are by providing your U.S. driver's license, non-driver identity card, or U.S. Passport. In special circumstances, when these things have been lost, you may also provide your employee ID card, school ID card, health insurance card, U.S. military ID, and/or adoption decree.

4. If you have changed your name since birth, you will need to provide documentation of that as well. This may include your marriage license, divorce decree, certificate of naturalization showing the new name, or court order for a name change. In addition, you must show identity documents with both names and recent photographs.

Every state has local offices so that you can contact the Social Security Administration with any questions you may have without having to drive all the way to their headquarters in Maryland. However, if you do wish to write to the Social Security Administration, their Office of Public Inquires is the best way to go. Write them at:

Social Security Administration
Office of Public Inquiries

Windsor Park building
6401 Security Boulevard
Baltimore, MD 21235

You can also call toll-free at 1-800-772-1213 between the hours of 7 a.m. and 7 p.m. Eastern time on Mondays through Fridays. In addition, recorded information is available 24 hours a day if you have a common question that you need to be answered. Note that when you call, you may be asked for your social security number to track questions. In this case, you can give it out without worry, although you should make sure that you are in a private case when reciting it over the phone.

A NOTE ABOUT DEALING WITH COMPANIES THAT DO NOT BELIEVE YOU

Sometimes discovering your identity has been stolen is not the end of your problems. Unfortunately, sometimes you will have issues dealing with companies who might not believe your identity has been stolen. It will be your job to prove your innocence.

First of all, if you are attempting to deal with banks or credit card companies that might not believe your credit has been stolen, you might feel as if you are fighting an uphill battle. The first thing that you need to do is make sure that you have kept your own very close records. Go through the bank statement and the online statements very carefully and keep track of everything that you see. Be sure that you are writing down and keeping careful track of what your purchases are and what purchases are not yours.

Then, you need to talk to the company about your situation. Even if they do not believe you, it is important that you remain calm and that your story is always the same. A story that wavers is not going to get you very far, so be sure that you are absolutely sure about what you have purchased and what you have not. Please remember that remaining calm is something that is always important.

The next thing that you have to remember is that each time your credit cards are used, there should be a record. Therefore, if your credit card company is saying that you made purchases that you did not, you have every right to ask them to show you the proof. There should be credit card receipts that show when and where the card was used. After you have these, there are several things that you can do. You can attempt to prove that the signature is not yours. You can also attempt to prove that you were not in the place where the transaction took place. If it was done online, you can also ask to find out what computer made that transaction, and then you can prove that it was not your computer.

These are all important ways that you can deal with a company that does not believe your identity has been stolen. It is most important that you are able to keep a calm head and that you have your own records for proof. You should also keep all of the proof that you find on your own, so that if you ever have problems with a company dealing with your credit because of your identity theft. You want to be sure that you are able to do these things right away. Keeping your own careful records is the best way you have to keep your own credit.

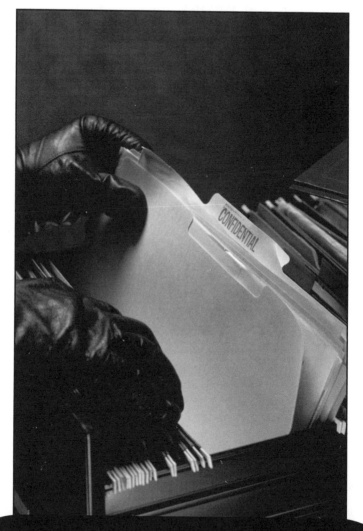

When you are certain that you are the victim of identity theft, try to find the cause and then report the crime to your local authorities.

SPECIAL CIRCUMSTANCES: WHEN FAMILY MEMBERS STEAL YOUR IDENTITY

Sadly, many identity theft victims know the person who stole their identity. While this is often the girl who took your order at a local restaurant or a neighbor who stole your mail, family members are also all too often the culprits. When someone in your family steals your identity, your finances may be ruined, but even worse, so is your relationship with that person. On top of that, it often causes the family to be split in two, as members of the family are forced to take sides.

For our purposes, we will consider close friends as family as well. In other words, identity thieves are often people you trust. One study in 2004 showed that over 30 percent of all identity thieves were relatives and an additional 18 percent were friends or neighbors. Again, the point of these statistics is not to scare you, but rather to suggest that you need to protect yourself even in what you consider a safe situation.

Computers give your family members (and friends) a whole new set of ways to steal identities. Whereas before an identity would have to be stolen the old-fashioned way – by actually taking paperwork, forging signatures, and otherwise stealing tangible items – computers and the Internet make it easier for family members to become identity thieves with just a few clicks. The result? More family members are turning to stealing identities because it is both easier and brings around fewer feelings of guilt. It might seem like a big deal for a son to go into his mother's personal belongings to steal her social security number, but it is not as big of a deal to look over her shoulder as she reviews her credit card account online.

PROFILE OF A FAMILY THIEF

There is no single sign that a family member is stealing your identity. It could be your teenage daughter looking to make some money or your jolly, laughing uncle using Thanksgiving as an excuse to snoop for information. It could be your grandmother or your grandson. It could even be your best friend or the person you trust to watch your children. Anyone who has any kind of access to your personal computer or anywhere else your personal information is available could potentially be an identity thief.

That said, a few characteristics are commonly found among family members who steal identities. None of these characteristics should make you accuse a family member of even considering stealing your identity. However, if you notice something weird with your personal information, keep in mind that you might want to look no further than your own home.

The Freeloader

Children and grandchildren are a gift from heaven. Well, maybe. There comes a point in everyone's life when it is time to fly away from the nest. Unfortunately, some parents (or grandparents, if that is the case) do not encourage or require this. There is simply something wrong with a 25-year-old who is still living at home and playing video games all day or who still gets all her credit card bills paid by mommy and daddy. The "freeloader" is the person who would rather have you pay for his or her bills than get a job or do anything worthwhile with his or her life.

It is not just children and grandchildren either. Have you ever opened your home to a down-and-out relative? We like to be nice to our family members, so when someone is in trouble, we all want to pitch in to help out. Let us say, for example, that your cousin's house is flooded in a major storm. You have a guest room, and offer to let him to stay while he gets back on his feet. But how long does it take to "get back on your feet?" Sometimes, family members take advantage of kindness and overstay their welcome.

And overstaying the welcome is the least of your worries. The freeloader is more likely to steal your identity, especially when threatened. This type of person is terrified by the fact that his or her meal ticket may be disappearing, and if you are threatening to "kick out" or "cut off" your freeloader, he or she may turn to desperate measures — like stealing your identity.

Freeloaders also have access to your identity. Most are not working or going to school while you probably are, so there is plenty of time to access your personal information while you are not around. Most freeloaders are not the kind that will sell your information for some quick money. Think about it; if you sell the identity information, that may get you a few hundred bucks today, but it still means that you are out on the street tomorrow. No, instead, the freeloader will look for ways in which they can take advantage of your information to fund their own needs. That might mean opening a credit card in your name or it might mean using you as a co-signer to get a loan where they otherwise would not have been approved. Your family knows you, so they are more likely to be cautious to avoid a confrontation with you. They will play it smart so you do not find out they are the one stealing your identity.

The Disgruntled Ex

Exes can be vicious. Whether it is a boyfriend, girlfriend,

wife, husband, lover, or just friend with whom you have had a falling out, your identity could be at risk. The goal here is to make your life as hard and as miserable as possible. You have wronged him or her in the past, so now your ex wants to make you pay. Unfortunately, this was a person with whom you used to be very close. That means that they know you and your habits. They may even know some of your personal information without even having to hunt for it. Exes can be very dangerous.

The further an ex can reach, the better. They want you to suffer. So, nothing is safe. Again, this family member (ex-family member, actually) will not just sell your identity to make some quick money. In fact, for exes, money usually is not the goal at all, unless there was a big settlement in your favor. Rather, your ex wants to waste your time and, over long periods of time, cause you financial hardship. It is common for an ex to do what it takes to ruin your credit in as many ways as possible. He or she has revenge on the mind.

Preventing an ex from using your personal information against you can be difficult. Again, it is common that he or she already has your social security number, driver's license number, and other sensitive information simple because, at one time, you were people who trusted one another very deeply. You may have had accounts together or have acted as co-signers for loans. It is very hard to go through the process of getting a new social security number, so that is not a valid route. After all, the government cannot issue a new social security number for every single person who goes through a rocky divorce. There are not enough hours in the day. So, you have to look at the situation as though your identity has already been compromised. What would you do if you thought a thief got a peak at your information?

First and foremost, if you have any accounts together, close them and separate your financial information. If you have a joint account and put $500 into it to pay your rent, there is nothing stopping your ex from withdrawing that $500, simply because he or she wants to go on a shopping spree. It is hard to prove that it was your money because it was in the joint account, so you may not even have a case against him or her in the court system. Instead, maintain a separate bank account. This is a good idea even if you are married to another person and very happy. You never know what the future holds, and having solely joint bank accounts is asking for trouble. No one is saying that you have to lie. Your spouse can know about your other bank account, and can even know the balance. So, for your own safety, keep yourself as the sole owner of the account. If something goes sour, you will have an account to fall back on without having to take the time from your schedule to open another.

When dealing with an ex, also make it well known to your attorney that he or she has access to your personal information if that is the case. You should call all three of the major credit reporting bureaus and request that your credit history be monitored. Close any accounts that you may have open and that your ex knew about because those will be the first places hit. Open new accounts with different lenders and different account numbers and keep this information personal. Be on guard, even if your divorce was somewhat amicable. Emotions run high and even if it was a mutual agreement to end the relationship as friends, do not take it for granted that the other person is ready to release you. You never know.

The Desperate Caregiver

Parents with young children and adult children with elderly parents top the list of family members who steal identities. When a caregiver is desperate, he or she often does things that would normally never even cross the mind. It is like cornering an animal. When threatened, even the sweetest dog will attack and bite you.

With a desperate caregiver, the victim may never find out that his or her identity is being stolen. There are two different kinds of victims in this case: children and the elderly. However, for both, identity theft can be a nightmare. A caregiver is supposed to be the one person you can trust even when the rest of the world is not safe. When a caregiver steals your identity, it takes a real toll on the entire family and on your own feelings regarding trust.

Children as victims — the world is a cruel place. Sadly, children are victims of identity theft quite commonly simply because, if their caregiver is not protecting them, no one is. A child does not understand what "credit" means. A child does not know to check his or her credit score annually. A child usually cannot even fathom why mommy or daddy would do anything bad to them. Child identity theft can be very confusing for the little boy or girl involved.

In mot cases with child identity theft by a family member, only one adult is involved in the actual theft. It is the other parent or a grandparent that usually figures out what is happening. When that happens, the child has to be involved to clear up the theft, but at the same time, emotions run high because someone supposedly responsible for the care of the child in question has essentially ripped him or her off. Children who have had their identity stolen may be placed in foster care or homes with distant relatives, depending on what the court decides when the problem is brought to light. It usually also causes a riff between spouses, and it is common for parents to divorce after something as major as one parent stealing the identity of a child and the other finding out years later. In addition, when the child is an adult and understands the implications of what happened, there is usually often a divide between the thief/parent and the child. It is hard to mend such a relationship.

Children may not find out that their credit has been ruined due to identity theft until they are 18 or even older. Usually, it happens when the child applies for student loans, a car loan, or a first credit card. The lender comes back with a crazy credit report that shows the child not paying insurance bills at the age of two or taking out a second mortgage at the age of seven. At that point, the real problems begin, and there are usually 18 years of problems to fix.

It can also go the other way. When we age, our children often take care of us, and that opens up more opportunities for a desperate family member to steal identities. It does not just happen with senile elderly people in nursing homes, either. Parents trust their children and take advice that they would never take from anyone else. Since aging parents do not always keep up with the latest technology, the Internet is a great opportunity for adult children to take advantage of a trusting parent. The children will set up accounts online, take their parent's social security number, and otherwise take advantage of sensitive information at their fingertips. When the parent says that something looks out of the ordinary, the child can just lie and say that the parent is mistaken. This creates a whole set of opportunities for dishonest family members. Remember, this can happen with relatives other than children. Anyone in the family can take advantage of an elderly relative.

The common thread here is desperation. When family members are desperate, they turn to scamming relatives — especially children and the elderly — whereas they would usually never consider the option. In most cases, it starts slowly. The thief is not an inherently bad person, just a person who feels like there are no other options. So, it will start slowly and the person will convince him- or herself that the theft is justifiable. How can identity theft ever be justifiable? Well, it should never be justified, but here are some scenarios in which you can see how a desperate family member would be able to convince him- or herself that what they are doing is "not that bad:"

- An adult son needs a loan to buy a car, but his credit

is not approved. He takes the money he needs for the down payment out of his elderly mother's bank account, justifying it to himself because he can use the car to get her back and forth to her doctor's appointments instead of having to take the bus.

- A parent cannot afford private school, so she uses her five-year-old son's spotless credit history to take out a loan. After all, the money is going toward his education, so it cannot be that bad to do that, even if she does not have the means to pay it back right away. She tells herself that, by the time he is 18, the debts to his name will have been cleared up and he will never know the difference.

- A grandson needs a loan from the bank to buy his dream motorcycle. His credit stinks because he was late on car payments in the past, and he will only be approved if he finds a co-signer. Using a card she sent him for his birthday, he forges his grandmother's signature on all the documents. He talks to her on the phone and also convinces her to give him her social security number and driver's license number, telling her that he needs to list that information on his college application since she is someone the school will call if there is an emergency. In no time, he has the bike, which he has a hard time paying for, ruining her credit as well as his own. He tells himself that it is no big deal, though. She is not going to take out any more loans before she dies anyway.

- A mother needs some quick cash for rent. So, she sells her infant daughter's social security number to an immigrant smuggler in town and he, in return, gives her $250. She justifies it to herself because the number is only going to be used by an immigrant to get a job, not for someone to ruin her daughter's credit, and hey, she can always "catch" the problem a few years down the road after everyone has forgotten she was the person who sold it. After all, the baby needs a roof over her head, does she not?

- When he was born, family members put money into a college account for a child. At the age of 13, the mother is having a hard time paying off her gambling debts. Since she is on the account as an authorized user, she pulls money from the account a little at a time. Twenty dollars here or there will not hurt, right? Soon the entire account is empty, but she keeps telling herself that she will put the money back soon. She is bound to "hit it big" at the slot machines sooner or later, and besides, her son does not need that money for at least five or six more years.

And so it goes with the excuses. They never end with the desperate caregiver. There is always a way to justify what they are doing, but the fact of the matter is that it is still wrong. The innocent victims are left without protection when their caregivers turn to identity theft.

Other Family Members

Do not fall into the trap of believing that your identity is safe even if no one in your immediately family falls in the aforementioned categories. Just like any stranger can be an identity theft, absolutely any family member can be an identity theft. Some do it because they like that adrenaline rush. Some do it because they know someone else that really needs the money. Others just do it for no reason at all.

Also, do not forget that "family members" includes people who are not living in your household. Do you fully trust the cousins who sleep at your house during the holidays? You must, if you do not keep you social security card in a locked box. Do you fully trust the babysitter? You must, if you do not log off of your computer and ensure that he or she cannot access the account you use where you passwords may me saved. Do you fully trust your brother's latest girlfriend? What about your best friend's son? Your housekeeper? Your grandmother's live-in nurse? All of these people are often left in house unattended with your unprotected personal information.

HOW TO CATCH AN IDENTITY THIEF IN YOUR FAMILY

One of the biggest group of people who steal identities are actually family members. This happens often with children – but it can happen to you too, especially if you leave your family information all in one place. All someone has to know is your social security number, and then can take out credit cards using your account. When this happens, your identity has been compromised. If you keep your social security card in the same place as you keep your child's card, you might find that it all gets stolen – and there are suddenly credit cards that are used by someone else. If this person is a family member, it might be difficult for you to confront them and catch them at the act.

The first thing that you to do is figure out who is stealing your identity. There are many ways that you can do this. Who had access to the information that they needed? Who was able to have this information? The best way to make sure you are right about who is stealing your identity is to double check the purchases and see what they have been doing with your and your child's identities.

Once you have taken care of this, you will be better able to have an idea of who might be stealing your identity. Then, you want to take a good look at how you can stop them for stealing it even further or from doing worse. The best thing that you can do to catch someone who has stolen your identity or your child's identity is to talk to the police about the situation. The police are usually going to be able to stop someone who has stolen identities, and they will also be able to help you get your money back. If you do not report someone to the police – even if they are your family members – you will find that your credit and your child's credit might be ruined. You want to be sure that you have taken all of the steps that you can to save the identity of your child. This is very important. If you do not take steps to make sure that the identity is restored, you will not be able to recover. You want to be sure that you are taking all of the steps, so that you will be able to restore the credit of the people who have had their identity stolen.

GETTING HELP WHEN SOMEONE IN YOUR FAMILY IS STEALING IDENTITIES

When you have discovered that a person who is in your family has stolen your identity or your child's identity, you are going to need to talk to someone. It might be hard to do – because when your family member has stolen something from you, it might seem like you do not want to get the police involved. However, it is very important that you do talk to someone, and that you do it right away.

The first person that you should talk to is the police. It might seem very extreme, but you want to be sure that you are talking to the police as soon as you can. You need to talk to the police because if you are not talking to the police, you will find that your credit is ruined. The police are the only people who can start an investigation, and who can make sure that you are able to get your credit restored. You have to be sure that you are doing as much as you can to get the ball rolling on the investigation.

It might be tempting to not call the police about identity theft because it is someone in your family that is doing it – and you might want to keep it quiet. When this happens – you might feel that you can simply put it behind you and move on. However, there is a problem if you don't report the identity theft. The biggest problem is if you and your child have had your identities stolen, it means that your credit has been ruined. This could be a huge problem. Your credit could be destroyed, which would mean that you would have problems getting loans, getting credit, and having other things happen. You absolutely have to make sure that you can restore your credit. The only way that you will be able to restore your credit is to report the crime.

Therefore, when you are dealing with identity theft, no matter who has done it or how close they are to you, you absolutely have to be sure that you are reporting the problems and starting an investigation. You want to be sure that you can do this because reporting it is the only way that you will be able to restore your credit.

It is especially important that you are contacting the police if your child's identity has been stolen by someone – even if they are a member of your family. Your child needs to be able to begin his own life with a credit report that is clean and clear and not in any problem. You want to be sure that you can give your child this type of life, and therefore you absolutely have to be sure to report any credit problems. You do not want your child to have to begin with any problems. Therefore, any stolen identities or problems have to be reported as soon as you know about them, so that you will be able to solve them.

Over 25 percent of identity theft victims reported that they knew or were related to the person who stole their identity.

IS ANYONE OUT THERE? IDENTITY THEFT PROTECTION HELP & RESOURCES

The future of identity theft looks grim. Three in four Americans are worried about the security of their personal information in the future – more than at any other time in history. Thieves are getting smarter. Technology is racing ahead, and many wonder at what expense. Are we prepared to deal with the problems posed in the future?

Identity theft is scary; there are no doubts about that. It can ruin your career, your finances, your personal life, and even your family life. Every year, thousands and thousands of people succumb to each kind of identity theft. That means that there are millions of victims all around the world, with new cases popping up every minute of every day.

One of the biggest problems with protecting your identity is that thieves are always changing the ways that they are able to steal it. Each day, it seems that there are brand new ways that people are having their identities stolen – and often it seems that some people do not know that how they have had their identity stolen – just that is has been. This is something that is a big problem when it comes to your own identity, because when you find yourself in identity theft problems, you have to figure out how it happened to you so that you know what you can do to avoid in the future.

There are many ways that you can be sure that you will be able to deal with the ever changing identity theft problems. First of all, it is important for you to be vigilant and keep track of all of the things that you have already heard about identity theft. You should keep a running record in your mind about how you should avoid getting your identity stolen. It is important that you are able to keep track of all of the ways that your identity might be stolen, so that you know you can prevent it.

The next step is for you to make sure you are always paying attention to the news about identity theft. This is important because every time there is a new scam, it will be reported. This is something that you should always know. As long as you are keeping track of the new methods, you will be able to avoid whichever ones you can.

Next, you want to remember that you are going to be your own best defense when it comes to the ever changing methods of identity theft. You should be checking on your bank account and other accounts as often as you can – once per day if possible. You should keep track of everything that happens with your bank account – and you always want to be sure that you are reporting any problems or discrepancies directly to your bank. You want to be the person who is keeping the closest track of their bank account, and this will be your best defense. This is the best thing that you can do because no matter what a thief tries next, you will be the first one to spot when something has happened.

It is very important for your future that you are able to keep track of what identity thieves and what they happen to be doing. Even though banks are getting much better about helping you regain your money and take care of anything that comes up – you still want to be sure that you are protecting yourself as much as possible. You want to always be sure that when you take your money into your own hands and that you are always able to save the money that you need to.

So what else can you do?

There is help. Although thieves are smart, there are some great resources out there that are, in most cases, smarter. You don't have to live in fear, wondering when and if identity theft will strike you. Prevention is possible, even if the ever-changing world of identity theft. In this chapter, you'll find all of the resources you need to continue your education, find professionals, and learn about protection options.

IDENTITY THEFT PROTECTION

Should you get insurance to protect you from identity theft? Absolutely. There are no guarantees. Even if you follow every piece of advice given in this book, you can still easily fall victim, especially if your use a credit car to make purchases over the Internet. Identity theft protection is insurance so that even if your identity is stolen, you don't have to pay for the problems resulting from it. With millions of people losing thousands of dollars every year to identity theft, you can't really afford not to buy it.

Each identity theft insurance program is a bit different. Which one is right for you? That depends on your specific wants and needs. In general, however, most plans are fairly similar and can be purchased for a premium of under $15 per month. That is less than $180 per year for, in many cases, up to a million dollars in protection.

When starting this book, you read about how putting yourself on the radar as someone who is interested in learning about identity protection can in and of itself defer criminals. Purchasing identity theft protection can do the same thing. Companies employ professional to bring thieves to justice, and they have a much farther reach than an individual has. Why get caught if you can steal the identity of someone who is not protected and, in theory, unsuspecting?

When comparing identity theft protection plans, there are a number of insurance features for you to consider. Looking at the following features can help you decide which plan is right for you:

- Monthly or annual cost

- Fraud alerts

- Credit report monitoring

- Credit score monitoring

- Insurance coverage against theft

- Assistance with recovery

- Pre-approved credit card stopping

- Internet scanning

- Ease to sign up

- Free trials

There are quite a few different companies offering identity theft insurance, with more popping up every day due to the prevalence of identity theft in today's world. Here is contact information for some of the older and most trusted insurance planes:

Identity Guard
P.O. Box 222455
Chantilly, VA 20153-2455
1-800-452-2541
8:00 AM – 11:00 PM EST, Monday – Friday
9:00 AM – 6:00 PM EST, Saturday
customersupport@identityguard.com
http://www.identityguard.com

LifeLock
20 East Rio Salado Parkway
Suite 400
Tempe, AZ 85281
1-877-543-3562
1-480-682-5130 (fax)
24/7 customer support
client.services@lifelock.com
http://www.lifelock.com

TrustedID
555 Twin Dolphin Drive
Suite 610
Redwood City, CA 94065
1-888-548-7878
1-650-631-8111 (fax)
7:30 AM – 4:30 PM Pacific, Monday – Friday
help@trustedid.com
http://www.trustedid.com

GREAT IDENTITY THEFT WEB SITES

It may seem ironic that the Internet is one of the best places to find information regarding online identity theft, but it makes sense when you think about it. Identity theft is changing so quickly that the Internet is pretty much the only way to get new information out to the general public very quickly. Here are some of the very best Web sites for identity theft information:

FTC's site on identity theft
http://www.ftc.gov/bcp/edu/microsites/idtheft/

Identity Theft Prevention and Survival
http://www.identitytheft.org/

Privacy Rights Clearinghouse
http://www.privacyrights.org/identity.htm

The Internet Crime Complaint Center
http://www.ic3.gov/

The Identity Theft Resource Center
http://www.idtheftcenter.org/

Fight Identity Theft
http://www.fightidentitytheft.com/

IDENTITY THEFT BOOKS

To take things even further, there are a number of other publications that can teach you the basics of identity theft and go into even greater detail about some of the things we talked about here. Remember, written books will be out of date fairly quickly in regards to the newest identity theft scams. However, these are a great addition to your identity theft prevention library!

- *50 Ways to Protect Your Identity and Your Credit: Everything Your Need to Know about Identity Theft, Credit Cards, Credit Repair, and Credit* Reports by Steve Weisman

- *Economics of Identity Theft: Avoidance, Causes and Possible Cures* by L. Jean Camp

- *Identity Theft: What It Is, How to Prevent It, and What to Do If It Happens to You* by Rob Hamdi

- *Insider's Secrets to Identity Theft: What They Don't Want You to Know (Insider's Guide)* by T. Carter

- *Investigating Identity Theft: A Guide for Businesses, Law Enforcement, and Victims* by Judith M. Collins

- *Johnny May's Guide to Preventing Identity Theft: How Criminals Steal Your Personal Information, How to Prevent it, and What to Do if You Become a Victim* by Johnny R. May

- *Pocket Guide to Identity Theft* by Lou Savelli

- *Preventing Identity Theft for Dummies* by Michael J. Arata, Jr.

- *Privacy Crisis: Identity Theft Prevention Place and Guide to Living Anonymously* by Grant Hall

- *The Rational Guide to Preventing Identity Theft* by Jerri Ledford

- *Stealing Your Life: The Ultimate Identity Theft Prevention Plan* by Frank W. Abagnale

- *The Wall Street Jounal's Complete Identity Theft Guidebook: How to Protect Yourself from the Most Pervasive Crime in America* by Terri Cullen

- *Your Evil Twin Behind the Identity Theft Epidemic* by B. Sullivan

An identity theft victim spends between 30 and 60 hours on average trying to straighten out the situation.

APPENDIX 1: FORM LETTERS

Dealing with identity theft? Here are some form letters you can use to contact the right people! A phone call or e-mail is great, but make sure that they have your information in writing as well – send it be certified mail so there are no disputes in the future.

DISPUTING ITEMS ON YOUR CREDIT REPORT

Date
Your Name
Your Address
City, State, Zip Code

RE: Inaccuracies on Credit Report

Credit Reporting Bureau Name
Bureau Address
City, State, Zip Code

Dear Sir or Madam:

Please be informed that I believe there to be inaccuracies on my credit report. The following items, which are circled on my report (see attached), are incorrect to the best of my knowledge:

1. Identify first item by name. This item is inaccurate because list reasons here. I am requesting that this item be corrected to reflect the accurate information. Enclosed are copies of name documents to verify that the information should be changed.

2. Identify second item by name...

3. Identify third item by name...

Please fully investigate these matters and correct the disputed items according to the Fair Credit Reporting Act. Inform me via writing of this outcome, please, and if you have any questions, you can contact me at phone number. Thank you for your timely response in this matter.

Sincerely,

Signature
Printed Name

DISPUTING A COLLECTION AGENCY CLAIM

Date
Your Name
Your Address
City, State, Zip Code

RE: Notice to Cease Case due to Identity Theft

Collection Agency Name
Agency Address
City, State, Zip Code

Dear contact person name or Sit/Madam:

I was contacted by name via phone call or e-mail, who informed me that you agency is attempting to collect amount on behalf of lender. Note case number if you have one.

I am a victim of identity theft, and the debt in question is currently being investigated, as it was incurred without my knowledge or consent. Enclosed is a record of this investigation.

This is a notice to cease contact regarding this debt except with information or questions necessary to clear my name. In accordance with federal and state laws, you may only contact me once more to verify that you have received this letter.

Also in accordance to federal law, under the Fair Debt Collection Practices Act, I am requesting that you forward copies of any documents you agency possesses as proof of debt. These documents may be mailed to the address above. Please let me know if you need additional information from me to close this matter.

Thank you for your timely and considerate response by date two weeks from mailing date.

Sincerely,

Signature
Printed Name

DISPUTING ACCOUNT CHARGES

Date
Your Name
Your Address
City, State, Zip Code

RE: Inaccuracies on Account

Creditor Name
Creditor Address
City, State, Zip Code

Dear Sir or Madam:

As per my discussion with name via telephone on date, I am disputing a fraudulent charge on my account in the amount of amount. I believe that I am the victim of identity theft, and am seeking your help in investigating this matter.

I ask that this charge be removed and that my account be placed on hold until this matter is resolved. In accordance to federal law, I also ask that you notify all three credit bureaus to correct the information on my credit reports.

I have already reported my identity theft situation to the local policy, the credit reporting bureaus, and list any other please here. Enclosed is verification of the ongoing investigation. Thank you for also looking into these matters in a timely fashion.

Sincerely,

Signature
Printed Name

APPENDIX 2: WHO IS STEALING YOUR IDENTITY ANSWERS

1.) If you said yes, you have been scammed. Mark Shae never died as Nancy claimed. In fact, their names were actually Mark and Nancy Dreksler. The Drekslers moved around three times in less than a year to outrun the cops, who wanted them on charges of fraud to the tune of over $110,000 in purchases with other people's money. The online community lost $60,000 in money and even more in free labor to "help" in her "time of need." They also ran a number of online auction scams in which they would use fake eBay screen names to auction off items they would never send.

2.) If you are the officers of MITS (Micro Instrumentation and Telemetry Systems), you agree and meet one of the most fascinating people you could ever imagine.

You hire young Bill Gates and are responsible for helping to propel Gates to his stardom today in the field of computers and electronics. If you said no, you said no to Microsoft.

3.) I hope you said no, because Scott Levine was indicted on 144 counts of conspiracy, fraud, money laundering, and obstruction of justice in 2004. He targets the company Acxiom Corp, stealing 8.2 gigabytes of personal data and costing the company and individuals over $7 million in damages. Scott and his company, Snipermail.com, were deeply involved in identity theft.

4.) Follow up on the mistake with each of the major credit bureaus and the federal government. In 2005, Steve Millet attempted to apply for a job at Target and was denied on the basis that he was already an employee. As it turns out, it was not a mistake. An illegal immigrant had purchased Steve's social security number and used it not only to get a job, but also to take out loans, pay taxes, buy a car, and open a dozen different credit cards. The person got away with the theft for over ten years by flying under the radar and making sure that he or she did not get too far into debt or otherwise notify the real Steve Millet of the problem. If Steve had not followed up, the case would have probably been swept under the rug, leaving it further ruining his finances for years to come.

5.) A woman from Missouri did, and he scammed her for thousands of dollars. When the date of his return came and went, the e-mail account he had been using was deleted, and he disappeared. She never heard from him again, and because she sent the money via wire transfer, there was no way to track who actually picked it up in Africa. For the price of a few teddy bears and balloons, the scam artist made big bucks — and broke someone's heart. In fact, he probably used the same scam and story on dozens of other women as well, although no one has ever been able to catch him.

6.) John Ozarchuck did, and four months later he and his now-wife, Christine, got engaged. Over two years later, the couple is still extremely happy and now has a baby. As opposed to the previous scenario, neither person asked the other for money or favors, and their date in real life helped confirm that they were both trustworthy.

7.) In 2005, Mark Anthony Kolowich and his Web site, World Express Rx, were shut down for running a business just like that one. He sold counterfeit drugs, most of which were unregulated by any kind of government and smuggled into the country through Mexico. The users of his site were asked to pay a small fee for review of their case, but there were never any doctors on the World Express Rx team. They approved everyone in order to make the most money possible. The drugs they sold were labeled as generic, but they contained very real ingredients, similar if not duplications of the ingredients found in drugs like Viagra, Cialis, Xenical, and Celebrex, among many others. Kolowich also offered to help other online pharmaceutical companies start selling drugs online, and as he helped to build an empire, a single site working under him could expect to make over $1.5 million in sales during a year or two. Meanwhile, the drugs people were getting were illegal, and some did not even contain the right ingredients, putting people's health at risk. Online drug companies simply cannot be trusted to uphold the same standards as real life businesses. If they do not require a prescription, stay away.

8.) If you did, you would be a multi-millionaire, because the person I just described was Larry Page, one of the co-founders of Google. Although his page rank technology can review Web sites with incredible accuracy and speed, this is not a program meant to steal your identity. It is simply a tool for searching online. When someone explains a new program like this, it is extremely hard to weed out the poor programs that will create insecure information opportunities and valid programs that can really be an asset to the Internet. Even worse, many people equate "computer expert" with "identity thief" these days.

9.) While the coach may mean no harm, do not release the social security number. Asking for such information through e-mail is always a bad sign, and what is worse is you have not been told how this information will be stored or in what cases, exactly, it will be used before you are asked. It is important to note that there have been cases of coaches, school personnel, or families of those involved stealing the players' identities, simply by logging online to the coach's e-mail address and looking up the numbers. As a concerned parent, you definitely should be suspicious. Instead of e-mailing the number, fill out a form in the presence of the coach, seal it in an envelope, and sign the seal. If the information is ever legitimately needed, like if your son is ever taken to the emergency room, the seal can be broken and the information found. However, at the end of the season, you should get the envelope back intact. That is the best way to ensure that your son's identity is not stolen.

10.) Of course, not every situation works out like this one, but scammer and identity thief Chalana McFarland pulled house-flipping scams like this for a number of years. The houses they showed were often not even houses they owned yet. McFarland would work with crooked appraisers to inflate the price of the house, and the inspections would be forged. They would "sell" you the house, wait for your loan to go through, and then buy the house for much less than what you paid them. After only a few months of living in the house, the buyers would find out that the renovations needed would add thousands and thousands more to their debt, and most people defaulted, leaving lenders with houses worth much less than the amount still owed on the loan. On top of that, McFarland would now have your social security number, credit information, and more, making identity theft possible. In the space of a few years, McFarland made over \$20 million — she was caught, though, and is now serving a 30-year prison sentence. That may be a good thing, but even though she is off the streets, hundreds of families have had their finances ruined and their identities stolen, and there is little they can do to repair their credit.

APPENDIX 3: CELEBRITY IDENTITIES REVEALED

---

1. Fatboy Slim

2. Kareem Abdul-Jabbar

3. Erykah Badu

4. Jackie Chan

5. Marilyn Manson

6. Ayn Rand

7. Dr. Seuss

8. Ted Turner

9. John Wayne

10. Rob Zombie

APPENDIX 4: CELEBRITY HOTEL ALIASES REVEALED

---

1. Angelina Jolie

2. Paris Hilton

3. Britney Spears

4. George Clooney

5. Michael Jackson

6. Derek Jeter

7. Johnny Depp

8. also Johnny Depp

9. Elton John

10. Brad Pitt

INDEX